The American on the *Endurance*

Ice, Seas, and Terra Firma Adventures of William Lincoln Bakewell

daughter

Elizabeth A. Bakewell Rajala

"Destiny, providence, or just highly unusual circumstances had led William Bakewell to *The Endurance* and his random travels had equipped him with the right skills to become an indispensable crewmember."

Rand Shackleton

Dukes Hall Publishing   ~   2004
Munising, MI 49862

Published by Dukes Hall Publishing
elizabethrajala@hotmail.com

Dukes Hall Publishing
832 West Onota Street
Munising, MI 49862

Library of Congress Cataloging-to-Publication Data has been applied for.
ISBN 0-9749134-0-5

Second Edition
Edited by Elizabeth Anna Bakewell Rajala

Manufactured in the United States of America

Dedication

It was William L. Bakewell's wish to dedicate this book to his beloved granddaughters who were his pride and joy.

William Lincoln Bakewell and Granddaughters

L-R: Sarah Ann Rajala, Grandpa holding Nina Kay Rajala and Mary Elizabeth Rajala

Preface
"A Man on the Bus"

By William Lincoln Bakewell

Each day as you ride to your daily task, may it be on the suburban train, the street car, bus or whatever public conveyance you may use; are there not others who with as it may seem, mechanical regularity always ride the same one as you? Do you not watch for them to get on or off at their regular places? You learn to know them by sight and as the months or years go by, you learn some of their habits or to know their peculiarities. With some you pass the time of day, and when you have a seat together you start a conversation. You learn to know where they work, if they are married or single, and also bits of their history. You in time think you know all about them, but do you? Would you imagine, that any of their past histories would be as interesting or exciting as some of the articles you read in your favorite paper or magazine?

Take that big man that gets on at Main Street, the one with the heavy tool bag. You know that he is a mechanic of some kind, and as he is rather a quiet man that is all you know about him. There is that small blond woman, the large brunette woman, the old watchman and a small dark man. It may be if the old watchman would tell you parts of his life that it would be both interesting and surprising.

Well, I am the small dark man who has been riding that bus with you for three or four years and I think that some of my past life will be of interest to you. Here you will find tales of the old lumber camps of Michigan, of work during the building of the last great transcontinental railroad, and of life on the old time sailing ships. You will read about my experiences on an Antarctic expedition, ranching in Patagonia, and aboard ships during the First World War.

Prologue

In June 1964 my father and I attended the 50th reunion of the Endurance Expedition in London, given by Lord Edward Shackleton, second son of Sir Ernest Shackleton. Six survivors attended this gathering and two others were living but in nursing homes: Lionel Greenstreet, First Officer, Alexander H. Macklin, surgeon; James A. McIlroy, surgeon; Charles Green,

The 50tth celebration of the sailing of the "Endurance"

L-R: Walter How, Dr. Alexander Macklin, Dr. James McIlroy, Lionel Greenstreet, Charles Green, William Bakewell, and host, Lord Shackleton

cook; Walter How able seaman, and William L. Bakewell, able seaman. It was an emotional experience for these men who hadn't seen each other in 50 years.

In November and December of 1999, I had the opportunity of retracing some of the Endurance Expedition of 1914-1916. On our Antarctic cruise we were never trapped in the ice but we did see monumental icebergs and experienced very rough weather: a Force 12 hurricane gave us a taste of what Shackleton and his men experienced on their voyage to South Georgia . By zodiac we reached Elephant Island, a small, barren piece of rock, with miserable weather and little shelter. We spent forty-five minutes there. It is incomprehensible how 22 men survived for nearly 5 months awaiting rescue in such a desolate, sea-ravaged place. It's impossible not to feel that a higher power was watching over them all.

While on this Antarctic voyage of 1999, one of the passengers produced a collection of sea chanties. To my surprise there was one called "Whiskey, Johnnie," a song my father used to sing to me when I was a toddler. The Endurance crew sang these songs to keep up their spirits through the long days and months of darkness and cold, and it reminds me always of their courage and fortitude.

> *Whisky made the skipper say,*
> *Whisky, Johnnie*
> *Another Pull and then belay.*
> *Whiskey for my Johnnie*

With the help of many, I have tried to put my dad's memoirs in a publishable form. I have footnoted the memoirs in many places. This was done to enhance and explain situations that readers may not be familiar with at this time.

Elizabeth Anna Bakewell Rajala

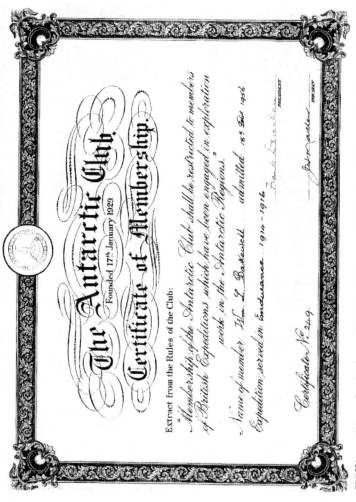

William Lincoln Bakewell's Certificate of Membership to The Antarctic Club

The American on the Endurance

THE ANTARCTICAN SOCIETY

The Officers and Board of Directors of The Antarctican Society,
after consideration of pertinent facts, have determined to award the
Society's Certificate of Recognition
to

𝕎illiam 𝕃. 𝔹akewell

who, in 1914, of his own volition joined the Imperial Trans-Antarctic
Expedition under the leadership of Sir Ernest Shackleton and thus became
the sole citizen of the United States to endure the hardships and
participate in the glories of that historic achievement.

President

Done in Washington, D.C.,
this *30*ᵗʰ day of *September* 1964.

Secretary

William Lincoln Bakewell's Certificate of Recognition to
The Antarctican Society

Bakewell, Ellen & Walter How—1964
Photo was taken at the time of the 50th Reunion

*William Lincoln Bakewell reading one
of the "Endurance" Books.*

Clockwise: ● *Document Wallet*
               ● *Polar Medal*
               ● *Palm Sewer*

Expedition Mementos

*L-R: Sarah Rajala, Mary Severson, Nina Rajala, and
Elizabeth Rajala*

The opening of the *Endurance* Exhibit at the American Museum of Natural History, New York City—April 1999. This was the first time the *James Caird* boat was on display in the USA.

Sarah, Mary, and Nina are William Bakewell's granddaughters. Elizabeth Anna Bakewell Rajala is his daughter.

L-R: Nina Rajala, Elizabeth Rajala, and Sarah Rajala, Alexandra Shackleton, Mary Severson and Alexandra's friend

April 1999—The opening of the "Endurance" Exhibit at the American Museum of Natural History, New York City. This was the first time the James Caird boat was on display in the USA.

The Endurance Odyssey Retraced
Nov. 26, 1999—Dec. 18, 1999

Elizabeth, Sarah and Nina Rajala sailed aboard
Akademik Shuleykin to the Antarctic. This trip somewhat followed the *Endurance* Expedition. We made
11 zodiac landings on our trip.

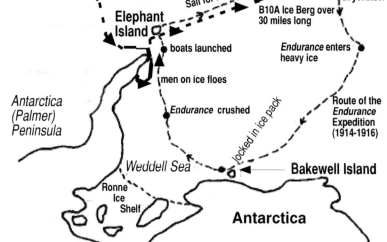

Note: The coordinates for Bakewell Island are
74° 50'S, 18° 55'W.

(Map by Jim Carter—from National Geographic and other sources)
Permission given to Elizabeth Bakewell Rajala to print.

*November and December 1999—Elephant Island
Sarah, Nina, Elizabeth, and the other
members of the cruise.*

Introducton

by Rand Shackleton

There were 28 men on board *The Endurance* and each one had a unique story of the circumstances leading to becoming a member of the expedition

Frank Hurley, deep in the outback of Australia, was given a telegram by an aboriginal runner. It was an invitation from Sir Ernest Shackleton to join the expedition. Frank Worsley dreamed he was sailing a ship down Burlington Street in London with icebergs floating all around. He went to Burlington Street the next day and found the offices of the Imperial Trans Antarctic Expedition and Ernest Shackleton.

William Bakewell seems to have begun his journey to *The Endurance* almost from birth. According to his mother, "from the time he could crawl he was out the door and down the street." At age seven he hopped his first freight train and at fifteen he left home for good in a frigid boxcar. He found work as a lumberjack in the forests of the Upper Peninsula of Michigan. At sixteen he made a solo five-day trek in sub-zero temperatures, through the dense woods to try to find an east-west railroad track. Nearly frozen and starved he came upon a train waiting on a sidetrack and was saved from expiring in the desolate forests.

He worked his way across the northern U.S. and Canada learning a variety of skills. Eventually, he found himself on the wharf in San Francisco where he talked his way onto a ship and began his training as an able bodied seaman.

Nine months later, coming into Montevideo, the ship struck the breakwater and had to be pulled for repairs. Bakewell and his buddy, Perce Blackborow, traveled across Rio de la Plata to Buenos Aires to find work on another ship. They got to the harbor just in time to find *The Endurance* getting ready to leave for Antarctica. Ernest Shackleton had just fired two crewmembers and was looking for someone to replace them. Shackleton hired Bakewell and his contributions to the success of their journey began. His first move was to stow his buddy Perce Blackborow aboard where he became an indispensable member of the crew. Destiny, providence, or just highly unusual circumstances had led William Bakewell to *The Endurance* and his random travels had equipped him with the right skills to become an indispensable crewmember.

Bakewell considered himself a common man and like most of the men who went through the experience of *The Endurance,* he rarely shared that story. We are fortunate that among his many skills, he was also a good writer. He had written this account of his remarkable life leading up to, during and after his experience on *The Endurance.*

Ernest Shackleton would be pleased that the stories of the individuals who became *Team Endurance* are finally coming to the attention of the public.

"Honor and recognition in case of success" was the first line of his famous recruitment ad. Thanks to recent efforts by numerous filmmakers and authors that part of the contract with his men in beginning to come true.

And thanks to William Bakewell, his daughter and granddaughters, his memoirs is now a historical part of "The Greatest Survival Story of all time."

Table of Contents

Chapter 1
Leaving Home for the Unknown

I left home [1904] when I was fifteen. I, like a great many other boys, did not care for school, and wanted the wide-open spaces. With less than a dollar in my pocket, and with the assistance of a few freight trains, and a lot of walking, I landed in the town of Seney, in the northern peninsula of Michigan, in the month of February. It was very cold and the snow was very deep.

Seney, Michigan Railroad Station

<u>Note:</u> In 1904, this is where my dad got off the freight train to begin his 20 years of adventures.

Seney at one time was noted as being the toughest town in the north woods, but to my surprise, I found it was fast becoming a ghost town. The lumbering in this area was finished, and Grand Marais, thirty miles to the north, had taken its place. While standing on the platform of the freight shed watching the freight train, which had ditched me here, disappear to the west, a man came out of a saloon across the railroad tracks and headed my way. I thought for sure it was the town marshal and that he would be after me. When he came, he said, "Hello kid, have you had breakfast?" I answered, "No Sir." He replied, "I am just going for mine, so come along." I was glad for I had not been eating very regularly since I had left home. I had a very good meal and then went back to the saloon with my host, a Mr. Harcourt. His name at that time did not mean anything to me, but some time later I found out I had been fed by one of the noted characters of Seney during its boom days. His brother had killed a man by the name of Dunn, who was a rival saloonkeeper. Regardless of what he had been, he was very nice to me, and by following his instructions, I got a job in one of the Ross Brother's cedar camps some twenty miles out of Grand Marais.

Lumbering in this area was in its heyday. This was a small camp and most of the men were Indians or half-breeds. They were piece workers, cutting ties, and fence posts. The wages were small, but there was plenty of work. I was given a job, driving an old gray horse, skidding the timber out to the main road. There was only one thing that the horse and I agreed on, and that was quitting time.

There was not much excitement in this camp. Most of the men were married and lived in shacks a short distance from the main camp. The only men living in the main camp were the teamsters and an odd piece worker.

While in this camp, I picked up an acquaintance with an old man, by the name of Potter. He lived in a shack a short distance from the camp, and was glad to have me come over of an evening. He liked to talk about his trapping and hunting, and I was all ears. On Sundays, he would let me go with him around his trap line. I would carry the extra traps and bait. It was through these Sunday hikes and evening talks that I received my first knowledge of the woods and how to trap the animals that lived in them.

I worked about three months in this camp. One day in early spring a big lumberjack, named Jack Webb, drifted into camp. He worked one day and quit. He told me that I could get better work in other camps, so I quit too. We went to Grand Marais, and there I had my first experience of a lumberjack's holiday: Red Squirrel Whiskey, wild women, and many fights.

My friend Webb had a grudge against all Finns. Some years back one had cut him with a knife without any reason, and since then Webb had been at war with all Finns. Webb was a very large man, about six feet three or four inches tall, active, and a good fighter. When he would go into a barroom, it was his delight to start a fight with any Finns present. All Finns who knew him would get up and leave. He would get me to knock over a Finn's drink, and when the Finn would start after me, he would reach out and with one blow the Finn would be on the floor, and as a rule all the fight was taken out of him. The Finn who would get up and go out was a wise man. Occasionally, one was not so wise, as he would get up and go after Webb with a knife. Webb would then get real mad and put the boot to him after taking away the knife and end the fight by kicking the Finn out the door. All the old lumberjacks disliked the Finns, as they had come into the camps and taken their jobs; therefore, Webb was doing them a great favor when he knocked out a Finn. As I was the instigator of many of these fights, all the men thought I was O.K., and I could have gotten away with murder. One day a Finn tried to knife me; he was a little too slow, and I knocked him out with a bottle.

3

Before I spent all my money, I bought a gun, as I did not care to meet up with a Finn when alone in the woods. There were also a great many wolves in the woods but my greatest worry was the Finns.

In a few days, I had spent all my money like a real lumberjack, and Webb had done the same. Considering all things, we had a swell time in Grand Marais. As our money was gone, we hiked out to one of the Alger-Smith camps.[1] It was a long day's hike. We made camp just before dark. As we were tired and very hungry, for we had not eaten all day, we surely did enjoy the supper that the cook fixed for us.

Jack Gleason[2] ran this camp. It was a pine camp. The real old lumberjacks would not work in any other kind. Those who worked in the other camps were hardwood savages or cedar savages, and were held beneath the old lumberjacks.

There was more excitement in this camp than in the other one. For one thing, there were poker games in the evenings. I was very quick to take an interest in these games. My partner, Webb, was so proficient at poker that he could not always get into the game, and I soon learned that if he was not in the game, it was better for me to stay out. I spent my time in the evenings teaching a Russian, who was new in the camp, how to play Pitch [a card game]. Webb was of splendid assistance to me, as he held a mirror from the top bunk, behind the Russian.

---

[1] Today Alger-Smith would be called a "holding company" as it was the parent organization for several operations. The company was founded in Detroit in 1880 by Russell A. Alger and M.S. Smith. Alger set up the Manistique Lumbering Co. to run his woods operations in the Alger County area. Gleason's camp was part of this operation. He also owned the Manistique Railway, which ran from Curtis, through Germfask and Seney to Grand Marais, which provided transportation for the logging business. Russell Alger served as governor of Michigan 1885-1886. Alger County was established in 1885.

[2] Gleason did a lot of cutting for Alger-Smith. His main camp was on the east side of the old Grand Marais-Seney Road (Co. Rd. 709), next and just south of the Grand Marais Airport. Its old foundations are still visible from the road. That area of pine forest burned over after it was logged, and is still referred to as 'Gleason's Burnings'

Note: Thanks to Jim Carter for the information concerning the Alger-Smith Lumber Camps.

We played for tobacco, and the Russian kept both of us well supplied and some to spare. The Russian was learning, and as he did not know that he had been cheated, all hands concerned were satisfied. The games were a source of real amusement for the rest of the men.

Before going any further, I will give you a description of an old time lumber camp. First is the office building where the foreman and the timekeeper live. It is also the commissary; here you will find clothes and tobacco for the crew. Second is the cook camp. This building is probably one hundred feet long and thirty feet wide. In one end is the kitchen, which occupies about twenty feet. It is equipped with two large stoves, several tables, a sink, dishes, cooking utensils, and miscellaneous items needed to prepare three big meals per day for a hundred or more very hungry men. The rest of the building is used for a dining hall. In it are two long tables, seating about fifty men each. Long benches on each side serve as chairs. Each man has his place at the table, and no unnecessary talking is allowed during the meals. It is eat and get. The cook is king of the cook camp and what he says is law. Meals are served on time, and you had better be there or you do not eat. However, if you should be late coming in from town, the cook will give you a lunch. Now as we leave the cook camp, we will look at the men's camp or bunkhouse. It is of the same design as the cook camp. You find on entering, bunks two tiers high around both sides and across one end. A long bench runs in front of the bunks and is called "The Deacon Seat." The deacon seat in front of each tier of bunks is the personal property of the men occupying those bunks. In the front of the bunkhouse is a large wooden sink with a number of tin washbasins and a long rack of roller towels. There are also several tables of one kind or another. Next, we visit the barn. This building looks very much like the others, and if it were not for the signs of horses, you could not tell the difference. Last on our camp description is the blacksmith shop. This building is about one half the size of the others. Let us stop for a minute and listen to the ring of the anvil as the Smithy swings his hammer and bends the red-hot iron, just from the forge, into any shape he may desire. There are runners for the sleighs, hooks, rings, and many other pieces of equipment needed for logging.

I believe that there is as much or more romance attached to the old time lumberjack as to any class of men that I have had the privilege of working or being with. This camp had a large number of the old timers. Many of them were in their sixties and a few were seventy and more. They or their fathers were from the eastern lumbering states such as Maine, New York, Pennsylvania, and others. In the evenings, they would sing the old chanteys, which were songs of a romantic or sentimental type. These songs told of the men who lost their lives on the big log drives on the Muskegon, or other rivers in Lower Michigan and elsewhere. After singing several of these songs, they would begin to tell stories; many were real thrillers and some were amusing. The stories portrayed very well the customs and things that happened in the old camps. One of these customs was, when a new man came into a camp, he had to sing a song, tell a story, or go up in a blanket. They also had this saying, "Of drawing in your Horns." This was used for any newcomer who boasted of what he could do, and when tested failed. I remember this story. One evening, a Canadian came into a camp down on the Muskegon River. He was sitting on the deacon seat in front of his bunk, when the camp bully, or Cock of the Walk as he was called, came up to him and said, "You must sing a song, tell a story, or go up in a blanket." The Canadian answered, " I cannot sing, I will not tell a story, nor will I go up in a blanket." As he put his hand back as if to draw a gun, the Cock of the Walk immediately backed away. Later in the evening, as they were sitting around the fire telling stories, the Canadian surprised them by saying, "I will tell you a story. Over in Canada where I came from, the pine trees are all ten feet in diameter and not more than three feet apart. We also have deer that weigh more than a thousand pounds and their horns are ten feet from tip to tip." There was silence. After a few seconds, the Cock of the Walk asked, "How do they get through the timber with such large horns?" "They draw in their horns, just like you did a little while ago," replied the Canadian, as he reached back as though to draw a gun; he pulled out a big red handkerchief to the amusement of all except the Cock of the Walk.

There were also the stories of Paul Bunyan, his famous Blue Ox, and the big Sleigh that could carry the timber off one hundred and sixty acres in one load. There were many other feats that Paul and the Blue Ox did, but it would take a book to tell all of the wonders they did, and one is already in print so I will not repeat them.

I stayed in this camp until fall. I learned many of the secrets of the woods, which since have been very useful to me. Many pleasant memories linger as I look back now fifty-four years, as I am writing this in 1958, and wonder what has become of those old timers. Many have gone over the Great Divide and joined Old Paul Bunyan. They were the last of America's great backwoodsmen, and I am proud now that I lived, if only a few months, with them. I left the area in December 1904. I had turned sixteen in November and now was a man!

Chapter 2
Chasing Dreams

In one summer I had changed from boy to man. I was small but very strong. I was like a piece of haywire and I could walk day in and day out, with my packsack on my back, and never tire of it. I wandered from camp to camp, working but a few days at a time. In between times, I would camp out along one of the many streams or lakes and hunt or fish. I surely was in my glory. Fall came and the leaves in the hardwoods began to fall. The Gypsy blood, that I must have a bit of, called me to roam again.

November came and the deer hunting season. I spent November [1904] and part of December in a deserted lumber camp, hunting and trapping. I will never forget the first deer that I shot. It was a fine big web horn buck. I sold it to an official of a railroad who had come up from Lower Michigan for the hunting season. I shot one more deer, a small spike horn buck, which I ate. I trapped mink and a number of muskrats which made me feel that I was a real trapper.

The old rambling fever soon had me again, and as I had heard some of the lumberjacks tell what a great place the Georgian Bay country, over in Canada, was for fishing and hunting; I was soon on my way. I crossed the St. Mary's River at Sault Saint Marie, Michigan, with Algoma as my destination. Algoma is on a branch of the Canadian Pacific Railroad, between Sault Saint Marie and Sudbury, Ontario, Canada. At Algoma, I picked up with three more wanderers. We made off down the tracks east to a place called Spragge, where the Shepherd and Gray Lumber Co. had an office. They were sending men back to their camp in the pine timber.

It took us two days to make the trip in a sleigh drawn by two horses. We followed the Serpent River, which was used as a road. We also crossed many small lakes. Winter was the only time that they could get in by team as the journey had to be made on the ice. It was a long cold drive, but I enjoyed it very much. It was after dark on the second day when we arrived at the camp. This camp was located on the shore of a fair size lake, which was drained by the Serpent River. The camp used the lake and river to float their logs down to their sawmill at Spragge. I was in for a big surprise, as this camp was far different from the ones I had been in before. About two thirds of the men were French Canadians, few of whom could speak English. The rest of the crew were old countrymen — English and Scottish. There was one other American besides me, a sailor from Boston. The French Canadians were from the eastern part of Canada. They were a very happy lot, and I got along fine with them. Every Saturday night there was a stag dance. They danced the old fashioned square dances, and the Frenchmen were very fine dancers. They would dance half the night, and longer if someone would play the fiddle for them. There was a great deal of horseplay among the Frenchmen. They did not bother any of the other men as they kept very much to themselves.

On Sundays, the Frenchmen would hold religious services that lasted about thirty minutes. The rest of the day they would spend in playing poker or mending their clothes. As for myself, I would be out hunting or on a lake watching some Indians, who were fishing through the ice. They had nets stretched under the ice by two holes in the ice, one at each end of the net; thus, they were able to pull the net in and out. They caught what to me was a great many fish, but they said fishing was very poor. The white men from the camp and the Indians did not have any use for one another. Whose fault, I do not know. I did not have any trouble with them. Being just a youngster probably had something to do with that. They seemed very poor, and they told me that game and fur were very scarce as there had been too much hunting and trapping. I became very friendly with one young Indian. His wife did my washing each week for twenty-five cents. I bought a pair of snowshoes from him and was not long in learning how to use them.

I had planned to go north to the main line of the Canadian Pacific Railroad when I quit this camp. The men in the camp said that the only way out was the way we had come in, but I had different ideas, and so far in life, I had been able to do what I had made up my mind to do. I had had some information from my Indian friend as to the best route to take and what to take with me. I had a very good compass, packsack, army mess kit, hunting axe, a big sheath knife, a small army pup tent, a 30-30 Winchester, and a 30-30 Colt. For an outfit, I thought this was pretty good. From the cook of the camp, I got about five pounds of flour, some sugar, tea, salt, a piece of salt pork, and some moose tallow or fat. He also fixed a nice lunch for me.

The morning I started my hike to the north was a clear, cold one in the middle of February 1905. Now as you sit in your warm and comfortable homes, this little journey of mine may not seem much to you. However, try to picture, if you can, a sixteen-year-old boy with all his worldly possessions in a packsack on his back and food for a week, the total weighing about thirty pounds, starting in the dead of a Northern Canadian winter for a place about one hundred miles away. The temperature was below zero, and there were no houses to shelter me until I reached my destination. You may now have some idea of what I was undertaking. As the song goes, " I do not know where I am going but I am on my way," so was I. From the camp I followed along the lake until I came to a small river that emptied into it from the north. I followed the river making very good time for the first two or three hours, then my packsack began to get heavy. I made my first stop in a clump of white birch trees, made a fire, and melted some snow to make tea, and ate the lunch that the cook had given me.

A typical lumber camp where I worked from 1904—1905

Credit: Grand Marais Historical Society—Michigan

It was frozen as hard as a rock; therefore I had to thaw it out before I could eat. After lunch I felt better and was again on my way, traveling until dark. The country was very rough, because of so many large black granite rocks (small mountains in fact). I followed the river, as my Indian friend had told me to do, for two days or until I came to a small lake, where I was to leave the water and go directly north through the hills. Then I would soon be down in the tamarack swamp country where traveling would be a great deal easier. The Indians had said that the railroad was a two days' journey through the tamarack swamp. This made a total of five days from the Shepherd and Gray camp.

My first camp was made in very short order. First, I made a big fire up against a large pine windfall; there was plenty of firewood at hand and it did not take much cutting to get it. I cut some small balsam and cedar trees. With these, I made a V-shaped wind break by laying first balsam and then the cedar brush. Next, I shoveled snow up all around this, using my snowshoe as a shovel. Soon I had a very snug shelter. I spread about six inches of boughs on the floor of my shelter for a bed, using the pup tent as a blanket. I also spread some boughs around the fire to keep my footgear from getting wet. For supper, I had tea and the rest of my lunch. After eating, I was ready to turn in, and did so with very little ceremony. With my mackinaw as a cover and my feet in the packsack, I was soon in the land of dreams. I slept well until awakened by the cold. My fire had burned low and with the temperature below zero and no blankets, I had to keep a good fire or there would not be any sleep for me. I had to replenish the fire several times that night. The night seemed extra long, and at the first signs of daylight in the east, I cooked my breakfast, which consisted of slapjacks[3], fried salt pork, and tea. At the same time, I cooked enough for my noon lunch.

---

[3] We would say pancakes, flapjacks, or griddlecakes.

It was not good daylight when I was ready to start, but I wanted to put at least ten hours on the trail that day. As my trail did not always go directly north on account of the many twists and turns in the river, I figured I was making about twenty miles each day. I saw my first game the second day. Three moose were crossing the river ahead of me, but I did not have any need for so much meat at once. Besides, I do not believe in killing for the fun of it. However, I was rewarded later in the day with a nice partridge. I made good time although it was bitterly cold. My packsack did not seem so heavy, but my rifle was some trouble as it was rather heavy, and my hands got so cold carrying it. At times I wished I did not have it, and I believe I would have left that gun; only I knew that I could sell it and would surely need the money.

The hills began to be more rolling and not so steep. The river was smaller and more crooked, and there was more brush along the banks. Around noon, I stopped to make tea. I was very thirsty and the only way to get a drink was to melt snow. The extreme cold, I believe is as bad to create thirst as the extreme heat. After my tea and slapjacks, I lost no time in getting on my way. I wanted to make the lake, where I would leave the river before night. About the middle of the afternoon, I had a very pleasant surprise as I rounded a bend in the river, I came out upon the lake. It was a tiny lake, in fact just a big pond, with brush all around the shore.

I took a bearing with my compass from where I stood. Looking due north I saw two hills, and between those I picked out another landmark farther north. From the last landmark, my journey was by compass entirely.

I felt fine as the directions that the Indian had given me were correct so far. I also was a bit ahead of the time the Indian said it would take to reach the lake. It took about half an hour to reach the two hills from where I was able to see a long way to the north. The hills seemed to run from the northeast to the southwest. In between the hills the land was flat, and the timber was tamarack and not very thick. There were many open spaces, and I surmised that they were very swampy; however, at that time they were covered with ice and snow. The timber in the hills was much smaller than that to the south. It was mostly pine and white birch.

Well, I kept plugging along until dark. I figured I had made about ten miles since I had left the river. I planned to make an early start the next morning thinking that I might be able to reach the railroad by night, but I had another thing coming. I made camp on the side of a hill near a clump of birch trees. The birch makes better firewood as it lasts longer than pine or tamarack. I was tired and very hungry, but I got my firewood first, then made my shelter and fire. I had a delicious supper that night. First, I cooked slapjacks, then the partridge. This I fried in moose tallow and when nearly cooked, I added some flour and water and let it finish cooking in the gravy, as this made it tender. I brewed tea, drinking it with my meal. None had to be forced down! If you are troubled with a poor appetite, just try walking twenty-five or thirty miles across country with the temperature below zero. I guarantee you will be able to eat and not be particular what it is. What you will want is quantity not quality. After supper, I was not long in going to sleep. I do not know how long I slept as I did not have a watch, but it had been some time because my fire had burned very low. It had started to snow and blow. I knew the weather had been too good to last. After putting an extra amount of wood on the fire, I rearranged my shelter and went to sleep again. At my next awakening, it was blowing and snowing much harder and was much warmer. The wind was in the northeast, and the wind and the snow would make traveling harder. I cooked my breakfast and had everything ready to start as soon as it was light enough to see.

I had to get to civilization soon, as my food was getting very low. Supper would finish the salt pork, and there was only flour enough for two more days. This was my third day on the trail and I was somewhat ahead of time. Traveling was difficult that day because of the wind and new-fallen snow. I kept going until noon and stopped just long enough to brew tea and eat a few slapjacks and a piece of moose tallow. I did not make much headway that afternoon because I could not see very far as it was snowing very hard, and I had to look at my compass more often. About an hour after my stop for lunch, I came to a large open space. I could not see across it, and it took quite awhile before I realized it was a lake. Then I remembered that the Indian had said there was a lake to the west of my route, about thirty miles from the railroad. I had traveled too far to the west. I kept to the edge of the lake and followed it to the east, as I did not want to take a course north which would have led me away from the lake. I had not traveled more than two hours when it began to get dark. It was still snowing, but the wind was not so strong. I stopped and made a camp on a small ridge where there was timber. I was not more than twenty-five miles from the railroad and should make that the next day. My supper that night was slim to say the least. I had just slapjacks, a little salt pork, and very weak tea. I must make the railroad the next day or have nothing to eat. I had not seen any game except the moose and the partridge. I had seen a few rabbit tracks but no rabbits and I had counted on shooting some to help eke out my food. It seemed that there was not any game moving. I had not even heard the howl of the wolves, although there were a great many in the country. I curled up by the fire and went to sleep, thinking of what I should have to eat on the next day when I reached the railroad. That night was the same as the other two: sleep awhile, then get up, and fix the fire to sleep some again.

The wind had died down by morning, but it was still snowing and my tracks of the night before were covered. I cooked the remainder of my flour and used only half of the tea and sugar for breakfast. I was on my way before daylight. The going was harder than ever that morning, as I sank eight or ten inches at every step, and it was snowing very hard; therefore, I could not see very far. One thing was in my favor. My packsack was very much lighter but I wished it were full of grub. I kept drilling along until I thought it was about noon. I could not see the sun, but that never-failing timepiece of mine (the stomach) said it was time to eat. I ate what I had left and drank the last of the tea, and as the last bite went down, I was on my way. As my next meal was somewhere in a northerly direction, it encouraged me greatly. It was the same old monotonous hike, and I still had not seen any signs of civilization. Just before dark, I heard a train whistle, and it did not seem far away. Night came on, and I kept going since it was the railroad or burst, and many a time I came near bursting when I fell over something my snowshoes found in the dark. I was just about all in when I heard the train whistle again, and then I heard the rattle as the train rumbled along. I knew I was not far away. I walked what seemed to me to be hours and hours. All of a sudden I heard a humming noise, and as I was standing between two streaks in the snow, I knew that I had reached the railroad; the humming I had heard was from the telegraph wires.

When Perry, Scott, or Amundsen reached the North and South Poles, I can imagine just about how they felt. I was where I had started for, and success is a great stimulant. I looked both ways and did not see anything, so I started west along the track. Walking was much easier as there was very little snow between the tracks. I was so tired that I could hardly put one foot before the other and it seemed a long time before I saw a light. One passenger and two freight trains had passed me going east and one passenger going west. Oh! How I wished I was on one of those passengers, just to curl up on a seat where it was warm, and go to sleep. The light I had seen was a red switch light, so I thought there was a town near but there was not, as I later discovered. A freight train came along and slowed down as it went in on the siding. I slipped off my snowshoes and caught the caboose as it went by. When I say, "I caught the caboose," I had better say, "I piled on," as the train was barely moving. The brakeman, who was standing on the rear end of the caboose, greeted me with, "What the hell is this?" It took but a moment for me to tell him that I wanted to get to a place where I could get something to eat and a place to sleep. I had the money to pay for it. He told me to go inside while he closed the switch, tell the conductor what I wanted, and he would fix me up. I was not long in doing what he told me. The conductor was as much surprised as the brakeman had been. I know I was rather an odd sight, with packsack on my back, snowshoes and rifle in my hands, and a liberal supply of snow on everything. The conductor very quickly saw what I was in need of, as he told me to put my snowshoes and rifle down and to take off my packsack. He then took a broom and brushed off as much of the snow as he could. By that time, the train had stopped and the brakeman came in. The conductor told him to get me something to eat (the train crew cooked their meals and lived in the caboose), which he did, and in the meantime I told the conductor where I had come from and how long I had been on the road. It was two a.m. when I got on the train, so that made five days on the trip, and blamed hard days they were.

They told me that if I had gone east when I reached the railroad, I would not have had so far to go before reaching a small town called Ramsey. They thought I had a lot of nerve and that it was a wonder I had not gotten lost, frozen to death, or eaten by the wolves. They also said that there was not a town of any size until we reached the division point, Chapleau, and that I could go there with them. They made a bed for me on one of the seats, and you may talk

17

about all your grand and glorious feelings, but when I stretched out between the blankets, it was Heaven. I have not the words to express to you how contented I felt during the few minutes I had before going to sleep. I was dead to the world until I was awakened at noon by the conductor with, "Lad, you had better get up and have something to eat as we will soon be in Chapleau." It seemed that the train had spent more time on the sidetrack, letting eastbound trains and westbound passengers pass, than it had in traveling.

The conductor wanted to know what I intended to do in the future. I told him that I did not know what I wanted to do, but if I could find work in Chapleau, that I might work for a while and if not, I would go further west. He said that he did not think I would get any work in Chapleau, because nothing was doing there but the railroad, and there were plenty of men for what work the railroad had. He also said that I would not find any work until I got west of Port Arthur[4], where I would again find the lumber camps.

I sold my rifle and snowshoes to the brakeman. He gave me fifteen dollars for them. I then had about fifty dollars and offered to pay the conductor for my ride and for what I had eaten. He would not take anything and after thanking them and bidding them goodbye, I proceeded to give the town the once over. It was not much of a place. I went to the Queen's Hotel and got a room. There were a number of men standing around the hotel, and I was not long in learning that there wasn't any work. I decided to rest for a few days and then go farther west.

Canada is a very fine country and the Canadians are nice people that are fun from Monday morning until Saturday night. The barrooms close at seven o'clock Saturday night and do not open until Monday morning.

---

[4] Port Arthur, along with Fort Williams, is now known as Thunder Bay, Ontario, Canada.

On Sunday, Canada is in the same class as a cemetery and the people seem to show they are living in one. They are so quiet at times, which I am of the opinion that they would be out of place even in a cemetery.

I arrived in Chapleau on Saturday and left Monday as one Sunday gave me all the rest that I needed. Monday morning I took a stroll down to the railroad yards to find out when I could get a freight train west as I did not want to spend any money on railroad fare.

While in Chapleau, I met one of the queerest pieces of humanity that I ever met. It was a man from London. He asked me if I could tell him how he could get a 'good's train' to Winnipeg. He also said, "I am bloody well starving." "Come on uptown and I will get you something to eat," I replied. He said, "I am starving with the bloody cold and not hunger, and I would like to have a good drink and get warm." "Come on," I said. In a nearby hotel bar I bought him a couple of drinks. With the effect of the drinks and the heat from a big stove, he became very talkative. He told me where he came from, where he was going, and why. He was a tailor, but had spent most of his life in the British army, with the "Dublin Fusiliers," and had been invalided out with a pension. He showed me his discharge papers, so I knew he was telling the truth. He had been in the Boer war, and if I remember correctly, he was in India and in the Sudan. He had been but a few months in Canada and had not been able to get much work. He wanted to go to Winnipeg where he had a friend who had a tailor shop, and who promised him work. He would also get his pension in Winnipeg, and he was greatly in need of it.

The queerest thing about him was the way he was dressed. A hard hat, a claw hammer tailcoat, a very bright colored vest, and pants that fit him so tight that he must have used a shoe horn to get into them. A pair of light pointed toe shoes, a suit of light underwear, and what I thought to be a stiff front shirt, was the surprise of my young life. It was nothing but a collar and front of a shirt, called a dickey.

Also he had a pair of cuffs that were held on by clamps fastened to his underwear. The dickey and cuffs were made of rubber or celluloid, and all he had to do to wash them, was to wipe them off with a damp cloth. This he did every day, if he had the opportunity. That certainly was a queer outfit in which to face a Canadian winter.

When I told him that I was going farther west by freight train, he asked me if I would show him how to ride, as that would be a new game for him. I said, "All right, but I am afraid you will freeze to death." He replied, "I will do the same here so I will take the chance." The only place that we could find on the train in which to ride was an empty stock car. Not so good, but beggars cannot be choosers.

I had on two heavy suits of wool underwear, two wool shirts, three pairs of heavy socks, a good suit of mackinaws, mittens, moccasins, and a cap. Therefore, I did not worry, but my new friend was not so warmly clothed and I did worry about him. I gave him two pairs of socks and a pair of moccasins. Say, did you ever see a Cockney tailor with moccasins on? Well, you do not know what you have missed. To top it all off, I wrapped the pup tent around him. He said, "I feel like a bloody Arab, and I am sure that Canada will make a blooming Hindian out of me."

Well, it was a very cold ride as we passed through about as cold and bleak a country as you would be able to find anywhere. We made a quick run to the next division point, White River, stopping just long enough to eat and get warm. Then we were soon off for Schreiber, which we made late in the afternoon of the second day. My friend hit some luck there. He tried to get work at a small tailor shop, but there was not any; however, the tailor gave him five dollars. I soon saw that he would not be satisfied until he had the money in circulation again. He paid for our supper, bed, and breakfast. This amounted to three dollars. He did not know how much money I had, as I had told him that I had only a few dollars.

After supper, we went into the barroom to get a drink, and while in there I saw one of the nicest little battles that I have ever seen. There were seven or eight men in the barroom drinking. With this group were four Englishmen who were about half stewed, and they were blowing about what they had done in the Boer War and how many Boers they had killed. My friend said to me that they were a bunch of bloody liars, and they had never seen a Boer in their lives. What started the fun was when one of them began to make fun of my friend's comic opera outfit. One word led to another, and soon my friend's nose began to get wrinkled and turn very red, and I knew there would be hell soon; I was right. There was a poker about four feet long lying under the stove. My friend walked over and grabbed it. "You bloody rotters," he said. "One Boer would kill a dozen like you. I have killed dozens of Boers, and now I shall show you how I did it." I thought that he would hit them over the head with the poker. However, he was holding it in such an awkward manner that I hardly knew what he would do. It took only a few seconds for me to see the surprise the Englishmen were in for. Before anyone in the barroom realized what was happening, he had two of them on the floor, each holding his stomach and moaning, and the other two were against the wall. He did all this by jabbing them with the poker. "That is the way I got my Boers, with a bloody bayonet, and here are the papers to prove it," he said. The proprietor came from behind the bar and said, "You have proven it all ready with that poker. Do not kill them as I think they have had enough." From then on, the drinks flew thick and fast.

Among the men in the barroom, was a railroad man who had been in the Boer War. He gave my friend some money, and told us that we could ride in the caboose of his train the next day to Nipigon. This surely was an improvement over the ride in the stock car. The conductor arranged at Nipigon for us to get to Port Arthur. This saved us a great deal.

At Port Arthur my friend got work, and wanted me to stick around; he would pay all the bills. This did not suit me, as I wanted to go farther west, so I bade him good-bye.

I made good time to the first division point out of Port Arthur, a place called Ignace. From Ignace, I caught a train that did not care if it went anywhere. I froze out early one morning at a place called Dinorwic. There I saw a great many teams, also sleighs which were being loaded with supplies, which I thought were for a lumber camp. Upon asking, I found it was the Hudson Bay Co.'s outfit going north. I tried to get a job, but they did not need anyone. One of the teamsters told me that a short way down the railroad at Wabigoon I might be able to get a job. After getting warm and eating breakfast I hiked off down the track for Wabigoon, where I found work but not what I wanted, however, better than none. The work was chopping wood for a hotel. This job paid twenty dollars per month with room and board. I had five stoves to supply. It kept me busy. I was not long in learning that I could increase my wages. I noticed that when a copper colored gentleman stuck his head around the woodshed and held up one or two fingers that meant for me to put one or two whiskey bottles in the woodpile. They would disappear in some mysterious way, and I would find two or four dollars in place of the bottles. I did a good business for about twenty days, when I got wind that certain gentlemen, who have this motto, "We get our man," had taken an interest in my wood pile business. So to keep them from adding, "We get our boy," to their motto, I left that night. I had become very much attached to that old woodpile. It had been very good to me, bringing in over two hundred dollars in twenty days. Nevertheless, the best of friends must part.

While looking over a freight train to find a place to ride, I noticed a light in a box car, and as the door was partly open, I went to investigate and found it occupied by a man with three horses, a cow, and other settler effects. He was going to Hanley,

Saskatchewan, to settle on a homestead. I asked if I could ride with him. He said, "Fine, if you will keep out of sight of the trainmen." I very quickly agreed to do so, and for the next four or five days all I did was eat and sleep. When we arrived at Hanley, I helped the settler unload his car. As Hanley was just a tiny place, I went on to Saskatoon. There I found more men than there was room for in the hotels. Here, I was with plenty of money and no place to sleep. I could not have been worse off if I had been broke. One consolation, there was plenty to eat. I bought some blankets and slept on the floor in the hotel office for a few nights at fifty cents per night.

I picked up an acquaintance with the man who was night fireman at the flourmill. He asked me to come and stay with him at night. I did, and with my blankets and plenty of flour sacks, I had a very fine bed. I was there about a month. Although the town was crowded, everyone seemed to have plenty of money, and they spent their money freely in the barrooms, yet there was not any disorder.

In Ontario, there was a great deal of snow, but in Saskatchewan, it was very muddy. This was the reason for so many men in Saskatoon. They were waiting for the mud to dry some so they could get out. Homesteaders needed to get to their claims and grading outfits to their work.

There was not much amusement in Saskatoon, but we did have one bit of excitement. One day the Mounted Police brought in a group of Doukhobors. They are a religious sect from Russia, who every so often roam around looking for the Christ. When they go on these pilgrimages, they disrobe. Men, women, and children are all as bare as the day they were born. It sure was a sight to behold and gave the people something to talk about besides the mud, homesteads, and the railroad work[5].

---

[5]Bakewell often related another story about his Saskatoon days to his family. Late one day a teamster needed to get his team of horses across the river. At that time, the only bridge was the railroad trestle. For five dollars, Bakewell led the team over that bridge, which was a dangerous thing to do with horses.

At last the ground thawed, and the roads dried out enough to be used. Everyone began to leave. I got a job driving a team for Foly, Lock and Larson, who had one of the largest contracts with the Grand Trunk Pacific Railroad. We went by train to a place called Langdon. From Langdon, it was a three days journey to where camp was made beside a big slew hole. The water was very strong with alkali and made many of the men sick. I was one of the few that it did not bother. The men did not stay long in this camp. Within a week or two, they were gone.

When the weather got hot, the mosquitoes were atrocious and kept both men and horses fighting them. I felt so sorry for the horses, as they had to work hard for ten hours during the day and then did not get any rest at night because of the mosquitoes. The grading is very hard on both the men and the horses, and the company did not have any consideration for either. That was one reason why I liked the lumber camps in Michigan. The companies there were good to the horses and the men were capable of taking care of themselves.

I might say that it took three crews to run the grading camps, one coming, one working, and one going. Each new crew of men was of a different nationality, and their queer ways were the only amusement that we had. One outfit of Austrians was like a pack of wolves. As soon as they were seated at the table, each man would grab the first dish he could get his hands on and empty it into his plate. If his plate did not hold it all, he would eat out of the serving dish. They ate like famished animals, and it was an impossibility to fill them. It was lucky for the "white men," as the cook called the Canadians and English-speaking element of the camp, that we had a table by ourselves. The Austrians did not stay long—only a few weeks—and we were very glad to have them go. The next group was Hollanders of whom only one could speak any English. He had worked a little while in England and had learned enough to act as interpreter for the others. They were all nice men but very green in the ways of the country. Their stay was the shortest of any. One evening the Hollanders created some excitement. Each one took a stick of wood from the woodpile and began drilling like a squad of soldiers, one man giving the orders. They kept drilling for about two hours. It amused the rest of the men very much, and we thought they had gone loco. The next morning there was not a Hollander in camp. Sometime during the night, they had taken French leave or shall we say Dutch leave. The foreman said he would remember that in the future, and if any group of Hollanders began to drill it would be a sign that they would leave before daylight.

The days were very long, and daylight remained until nine or ten o'clock in the evening. I did not blame any of the men for quitting, as it was very disagreeable work. When the wind would blow, we would be working in a cloud of dust, and when there was not any wind, the mosquitoes tried to devour us. I stuck it out until sometime in August of 1905.

From there, I went to Edmonton, Alberta. In Edmonton, I soon had most of the money that I had accumulated in circulation and was looking for work again. I found a job about five miles from Edmonton, at a small sawmill, which was owned by a man formerly of Missouri. I worked there four days. The owner's wife did the cooking and the two main articles of food were radishes and cottage cheese, which she served three times a day. What other food she put on the table was in such small quantities, that we were still hungry when we were through eating. All that would be left were a few radishes and some cottage cheese. That diet may have been fine for anyone wishing to reduce, but I was not of a build that needed reducing. I left and went back to Edmonton.

Excepting farm work, which I did not want, there was nothing to do but to go back to a grading camp. I shipped out that same day to a grading camp in eastern Alberta, about thirty miles south of Vermilion. Alberta is a much better country than Saskatchewan. The latter is what is known as bald face prairie and the former a park country. A Swede, who was a subcontractor under Foley, Lock and Larson, ran this camp. I only stayed there a few days. I got into an argument with the dump boss about where the dirt was to be dumped. He said something to me in the Swedish language, and as I happened to understand what he said, and it not being very complimentary, I knocked him down and over the dump. The dump boss was a nephew of the man who was in charge of the camp; therefore, I asked for the few dollars that were coming to me and quit. I started west, following the survey stakes, and trusted that luck would throw something my way. I came to the Battle River after about four hours, and there I found an engineer's camp. They were surveying for the bridge that the railroad was to use in crossing the river. I asked them for a job but they did not need anyone. The chief engineer told me that there was a man clearing brush along the right of way, some five or six miles farther west, and that he wanted someone to help him. I forded the river, which was about knee deep, and it was not long until I found the man I was looking for. He seemed glad to see me as he had been there for sometime alone; he was pleased to have someone to talk to. He was a young man in his early twenties, a Canadian from eastern Ontario. I told him that the surveyor had sent me to see about work, as I was in need of a job. The young man replied, "You have found it."

It was late in the day, so he stopped work and we went to his camp and soon had supper. After supper, we settled on what wages I was to receive. He had an eight by ten tent in which we both slept. He had about ten days more work to do on the station where he was working, and then he would get paid. He told me that if we worked well together, and if I wanted to, we would go into partnership on the next stations, which were under a different engineer.

Jim Collins was the name of my new partner, and a more square or better man never lived. Consequently, we got along and worked together until the latter part of October, when Jim had to go to his homestead in Saskatchewan and put in the required time needed to remain as owner of the place.

I worked all winter by myself, and after Jim left, I built a small shack in about the center of the work I had to do. This work covered about six miles, and the brush was in patches. Some of the brush came only a short way on to the right of way, and at other places it was quite thick all over the right of way. I was paid by the station, which is usually one hundred feet long by two hundred feet wide. This made almost a half-acre in each station. Some days I would clear three or four stations, and then some stations would take me several days to clear. I was paid twelve dollars and fifty cents per acre, so I made very good money for a kid. I worked every day until the last of March 1906, when I finished my work. I also did a little trapping and made as much as I would have had I been working in one of the camps.

I made only one trip out for supplies and mail. That was at Christmas time as I was expecting mail and presents from home. I went to Battle River crossing, where quite a settlement had sprung up in a few months. A store, restaurant, and numerous other outfits were there to accommodate the men who were working on the new bridge.

On this little trip, I had the only wolf scare of my life, and I have put in a great deal of time in countries where wolves were plentiful. I left my shack with just my packsack, because I wanted to carry back as many supplies as possible. Thus I did not take my gun. The only thing I had in the shape of a weapon was a large sheath knife with a seven-inch blade, which I always carried. When about two-thirds of the way to the settlement, I heard wolves howling to the north, and as the short winter day was ending, I did not exactly like it. Game was not very plentiful, so I did not exactly like it. I knew that the wolves would tackle a man, and naturally, I did not like the thoughts of being meat for them. Right there, I swore that I would never be without my gun again. Night was upon me, and I had about a mile to go. The trail led down a draw, which came out at the river and near the settlement. I had not heard the wolves howl for some time and had forgotten them. I was thinking of the good supper that I would soon get when all of a sudden, right in front of me, I spied eight or ten objects. Wolves, of course, were the first things that ran through my mind, and what could I do? There was no use going back as they would get me before I went very far. To stay where I was or go ahead would have had the same results. It took me only a few seconds to decide to go ahead. I took off my packsack, held it by the strap in my left hand, and held my sheath knife in the right hand. I advanced prepared for one big battle. I thought I might be able to bluff them with the packsack, and if I could get a chance to knife one he would know it. The closer I got the bigger they looked, and I imagined I could see their eyes. Still closer they looked more fierce, and the less I cared for the fight with them. Just as I expected them to spring, they changed their shape and wolf like appearances, and there stood eight or ten poplar stumps. Someone who did not believe in the conservation of timber had cut the stumps three feet above the ground. You may well imagine that I was glad they were stumps. No, I did not tell anyone in the settlement about it or anyone else for a long time.

I went to the store as soon as I arrived at the settlement to see if there was any mail. The man that ran the store brought the mail from Hardisty, a town twenty-five miles south on the Canadian Pacific Railroad. There was mail and a box for me. I bought what supplies I needed, loaded them in my packsack, and went to Windy Bob's restaurant for supper. While eating supper, I read my mail.

There were three other men staying at Windy Bob's that night. They were freight teamsters and had been on the road all day, and like me, they were very hungry and tired. Very soon after supper we all hit the hay and were soon off to dreamland until morning. I had breakfast at six o'clock and was on my way back to my shack by seven. My packsack weighed some fifty pounds. I did not feel the weight at first, but before I reached the shack, it felt as if it weighed a ton. My tracks of the day before made traveling much easier. I made very few stops for rest as I wanted to reach the shack before dark. I got there just at dark, and I was very tired, thirsty, and hungry. I soon had a fire made and water heating for tea. I opened the box that I had received from home and found candy, cigars, and a number of good things that they have back in God's country. The thing that took my eye was a large fruitcake. I immediately cut into the cake and made my supper of cake, candy, and tea. I must have eaten two or three pounds of the cake, and I do not know how much candy. It was the first I had had for two years, and I sure made up for lost time. After I had eaten all I could, I rolled into my bunk and was soon fast asleep. How long I slept I do not know. What felt like someone trying to kick my stomach to pieces awakened me. You talk about a stomachache: I had the king of them all. I thought I was going to die. It kept up until daylight when nature, at last, came to my relief. I was not long in coming to the conclusion that fruitcake and candy were not a proper diet. The rest I ate in smaller portions with my regular meals of pork and beans.

The rest of the winter soon passed with nothing of any importance happening. Just working, eating, and sleeping. I finished cutting the brush the last of March, and as my grub was nearly gone, I went back to Battle River Crossing to wait until the engineers came. That would be about the first of May. I shipped my furs to Edmonton to a fur buyer and planned to take things easy until I received the returns from the furs, and the return of the engineers, as they paid for the cutting of the brush.

I had been in Battle River only a few days when a man, who was hauling freight from Hardisty to Battle River with ox teams, asked me if I would drive one outfit. He had three freight wagons and used four oxen to each wagon. I took the job, and let me say here, that if you have never driven oxen you have fortunately missed great trials and tribulations. Moreover, as for increasing a person's vocabulary, driving oxen beats anything I ever run up against. You learn words that are not even in the dictionaries. If you wish to see the countryside, get a job driving oxen and you will have plenty of time to explore any part you cover; however, how much you cover is another question as the oxen have a way all their own, and believe me it is a slow way. It took us five days to make the return trip of fifty miles. I made six trips.

When the engineers returned, they measured my work and paid me. I also had the returns from the furs, quite a lot of money for an eighteen-year-old kid. I went immediately to Edmonton, the nearest place where I could put the money into circulation again. I stayed but a few days in Edmonton and then went to Calgary. The rambling bug had me again, so from Calgary, I went to Moose Jaw and then back to God's country. This time it was St. Paul and Minneapolis. When I came to my senses and the end of my finances, I was in Miles City, Montana.

.

Chapter 3
Montana Days

With the last few nickels that I had, I explored Miles City and found that I liked it very much and decided to stay for a while. I was in town only a few hours when I found work helping to halter break horses in the stockyards. Miles City at that time was one of the largest horse markets in the world. The German government had bought the horses that we were breaking. It was hard work yanking a horse around all day. As a rule, we broke only four per day. We had a great deal of fun and excitement and that more than paid for the hard work. The only fault I found was that the work was not steady. We worked only three or four days and then would be idle three or four. Consequently, I was broke all the time.

Miles City was a wide-open town, and the barrooms were open day and night. One morning while eating my breakfast in the restaurant at the back of the Silver Dollar Saloon, I began to talk with another man who was also eating. He asked me if I knew of anyone who wanted to work on a ranch. I told him that I did as I was looking for that kind of work. He said, "You are hired." In less than an hour, I was seated on a freight wagon behind six horses bound for Jack Milroy's ranch eighty miles north of Miles City. It took us three days to reach the ranch.

This area was very different to any I had been in before. Every few miles it would change from level prairie or sagebrush flats to rolling prairie, then a stretch of badlands. The badlands were what interested me the most. They are the results of ancient mud volcanoes and are made up of peaks, or "buttes" as they are called in Montana. They consist of small canyons, dry creeks and a general broken surface caused by erosion. Some people call the badlands the roughest and most desolate country in the world. To me it did not seem so, as each different formation gave me something to think about.

Jack Milroy's ranch was situated on a little creek about a mile from where this creek emptied into the Little Dry River. In the dry season, there was not much water excepting in holes, but in the spring or after a heavy rain, this little creek was a raging torrent. About a quarter of a mile from the ranch house, five children met us. Jack had seven children. The other two were too small to run so far or they would have been with the bigger ones. We stopped and let them get into the wagon. They were naturally very pleased to see their father, but I was given sideways and stolen glances. They were very shy with strangers, and for a while I was looked upon with suspicion. We quickly became acquainted, and from then on until I left the ranch, they were my constant companions. When I was working around the ranch, they were always close by. If I went anywhere with the team and wagon, I had a load of kids. If I were riding a horse that would carry more than one person, one, two, or three of them would pile on. The rest would be standing by crying because they could not come. I was just one of the family to them. All their troubles were shared with me, and we all had lots of sympathy for each other.

I will never forget the time I took the three oldest boys swimming in one of the water holes in the creek. It was an unearthly hot day in August of 1906. The water was only about two and one half feet deep. Our backs were exposed to the sun most of the time, and four more sunburnt backs I never saw. That night our backs were so sore that their mother put fresh cream on all of us. The kids naturally shed tears and when their mother criticized them for crying, saying, "Look, Bill is not crying." "No," one of them replied, "but I bet he wishes that he was little so he could." He certainly was speaking the truth.

32

Work on a sheep ranch is periodic. Some seasons of the year, work keeps one going practically day and night. Then for long spells there is nothing to do. Once a week I had to take supplies to the herder, and the rest of the time, I was hauling wood from along the river or digging lignite coal from a nearby bank. There were many days that I did not have any work to do, and it was during those days that I did my exploring. In a year's time, I knew every corner and nook for miles around. Day or night and even in some of the worst blizzards, I could find my way. My knowledge of the country came in handy many times when I was caught out at night or in a blizzard.

The nearest post office was a place called Cohagen. It was a ranch on the stage road twenty-five miles across country. That meant a fifty-mile ride in one day and over very rough country. I will never forget one trip that I made to Cohagen. I left the ranch early one morning. The weather was fine and clear. When I arrived at Cohagen a blizzard was raging, I gave my horse a good feed, and I had a good dinner and prepared for the return trip. The people of Cohagen begged me not to start as they were sure I would not be able to make it, but as I knew it was very important for me to get back to help with the sheep, I started back to the ranch. My horse was a large lanky beast, and as I had traveled over the same route many times with him, I knew he could find the way home. As I could only see about one hundred feet ahead, I did not try to guide my horse but let him go his own way. By some familiar objects, such as a knoll or gully, then a dry creek, I was able to check up on him and in that way satisfy myself that we were on the right trail. I reached the ranch safely, only to get a good bawling out from my boss. He said that if ever I should get caught out again like that, that I should make for the nearest shelter and never mind about the sheep as my life was worth more than the sheep. I said nothing to him but to myself I said, "I will do as I damn please." I was able to take care of myself and did so under some very trying conditions.

33

Photo permission given by Lynne Hadley & Jack McRae
L & L Hadley <amitie@bigpond.com>
jmcrae@midrivers.com

Montana Rancher, Jack (John) Milroy and Family Probably taken in 1904 or before. They had seven children when my dad was there in 1906.

Note: 1910 census shows a new baby making eight children. William Lincoln Bakewell is listed with the family on the 1910 census.

My next good bawling out from the boss was in the following spring [1907]. I had found a wolf den at the head of a draw or washout. I could see the wolf tracks leading to the hole in the bank. I did not get off my horse but went directly back to the ranch and got a pick, shovel, a bottle of kerosene, and some rags. The boss was not at home, so his oldest son, John, a lad of twelve or thirteen, accompanied me. We were both very excited. This was my first experience with a wolf's den. I had heard how other men had dug them out, crawled into the dens, and killed the old wolves. Naturally I was very excited over the prospects of the adventure.

When we got back to the den, the first thing that I did was to look and see which way the freshest tracks led, either in or out. There were so many tracks that I could not tell. I sailed in with pick and shovel; John eagerly helping all he could. After digging four or five feet, the hole was large enough for me to crawl into. I thought I would investigate and see what was in there. I plugged my ears with some pieces of rag, made a torch with rags and kerosene, and with the torch in one hand and my six shooter in the other, I proceeded to worm my way into the den. When I got about the length of my body into the hole, I heard an unearthly snarl, and a few feet ahead of me I saw two coals of fire. I waited for no more but fired three shots in the direction of the two coals of fire and did a backward wiggle out. I was nearly blinded from the smoke of the torch and the powder, my ears were ringing and felt like they would burst. My heart was going bump, bump, bump, and it was minutes before I could answer any of the hundred and one questions that my helper was asking. I waited probably thirty minutes, until the smoke ceased coming out of the hole. By that time I had myself together and had mustered up nerve enough to go back into the den and find out what damage I had done. I proceeded as before but I took along a rope. Upon entering this time, I was not greeted with a snarl and found the old wolf stretched out ahead of me, her head lying in a pool of blood. I very cautiously slipped the rope around her neck and crawled out. The two of us pulled out the wolf. She was a very large old brute. I do not know which was the most excited, the boy or I. I had to go back and get the pups. There were seven, and they were not more than a week or ten days old. I skinned the old wolf and put the pups into a bag, and then, two very proud wolf hunters started home. I was covered with dirt and blood but very happy. When we arrived at the ranch, it was suppertime. The boss, his wife, and the children were sitting out in front of the house watching for us. When they saw that I was all covered with dirt and blood, they began to ask all kinds of questions, all talking at the same time. John told them the story. The boss was pleased that we had gotten the wolves, but he did not like the risk that I had taken. He told me never to take a chance like that again unless there was another man along. In case of an accident, such as the hole caving in on me and

Milroy Storage Shed (photos taken in 2002)

Permission given by Lynne Hadley & Jack McRae to use the above photos.
L & L Hadley <amitie@bigpond.com>
jmcrae@midrivers.com

Milroy Ranch Bunkhouse (photos taken in 2002)

rendering me helpless, a boy might not know what to do. I promised I would not. I intended to keep the pups, but the boss would not listen to it. He took them by the hind legs and knocked their heads against a fence post. John and I protested but he would not let them live. He paid me the bounty and took the scalps to town. He received credit for them but had to wait sometime for the money as the bounty appropriation was used up.

The next excitement I had outside of regular ranch routine was with a pony that had been given to John. It had never been broken, and I wanted to ride it, but the boss was afraid that I would be thrown and hurt. I had to wait until he was away. My chance came soon. The boss left for Miles City with a load of wool. It would be seven or eight days before he would be back. There was not much for me to do, so I took advantage of his absence. The pony was a pretty, little sorrel mare, weighing about eight hundred pounds. She was slim built, like a miniature thoroughbred racehorse. I got her in the corral and did not have much trouble getting my saddle on her. I led her around the corral a few times,

Photo permission given by Lynne Hadley & Jack McRae
L & L Hadley <amitie@bigpond.com>
jmcrae@midrivers.com

Milroy Ranch Corral

and then mounted her. She gave but three jumps and quit. I was glad, for one more jump and I would have gone over her head. She never offered to buck after that. I rode her every day until she was bridle wise. John would go with me riding another horse. She was very gentle, and John wanted to ride her, but I was afraid to let him. I did not mind taking chances myself but did not like taking any chances of John getting hurt. On the sixth day, after the boss left, John rode the horse. His mother said it would be all right as she had witnessed all our maneuvers, and she felt sure the horse was safe for him to ride. I do not believe I have ever seen a boy as happy as John was when he got on that pony. He had a smile from ear to ear, and I think that the pony realized it as she was sure on her good behavior.

The eighth day, John's dad returned. We met him a mile from the house. He was pleased that the pony was broken and so gentle. John told him that the pony had bucked all around the corral for half an hour, and he was sure I could ride any horse alive. I knew differently but said nothing. During the summer, I bought a horse from Van Norman, who had a small ranch down where the Big and Little Dry Rivers meet. The horse had not been broken but I was confident that I could ride him. When I tried to put the saddle on him, I soon found out that I did not have the little mare to deal with. He bucked it off as fast as I could put it on. I tied his head to the snubbing post in the center of the corral and then managed to get the saddle on. When I untied him, he sure did some bucking, trying to get the saddle off. I was sure glad that I was not on him, for I know I could not have stayed on very long. When he became tired of trying to buck the saddle off, I thought he was all in and it would be a good time for me to try my luck. I had no trouble in getting on him, but to stay on was where the fun began. I managed to stay with him for a few minutes but he got me loosened and threw me clear over the corral fence. I landed on my feet and except for a few bruises I was all right.

However, I was sure angry, and I climbed back into the corral and made up my mind that no horse should get the better of me in that way and get by with it. I mounted and he went to bucking again for all he was worth, but I had better luck. He sure made me pull leather, but I stayed with him. I rode him until I could not make him buck any more and then took him out of the corral. John came along on his pony to help haze him along. I rode him for a couple of hours before turning him loose. The next day I gave him another good try out, but he never became as gentle as the little mare. He would buck every time he was ridden. I named him Buck and eventually sold him at a good profit.

The next bit of fun that I had was with a young Scotsman, who was herding sheep. Whenever he managed to get into the ranch, he was sure to play some trick on me such as putting water in the bunkhouse lamp or mixing pepper with my tobacco. I was just waiting to get back at him. My chance came one very dark night late in the fall [1907]. He had left the sheep sheds, which were about a mile from the ranch house and come to the house to spend the evening. Duncan (that was the herder's name) had been in the country less than a year. He was terribly afraid of getting lost in the dark, and I had loaded him up with wolf stories, so much so as to almost scare the wits out of him. That night was an extremely dark one, as there was no moon. I figured that it would be a fine time to give Duncan a good scare, and get back at him for the tricks he had played on me. Duncan had left a lantern burning on top of his wagon and another one on a hilltop half way between the wagon and the ranch house. By this, he would be able to keep a light always in sight, and he would not go astray. That night in the bunkhouse, the boss and I sure excelled ourselves in wolf yarns, and it was surprising how many instances that we knew of sheepherders getting lost and falling prey to the wolves. When it came time for Duncan to leave, the boss told him to come to the house, and he would give him some papers to take back with him. Duncan was very fond of reading, so he went to the house after the papers, and in the meantime, I was going as fast as my legs would carry me to Duncan's wagon. I took the light from the wagon and moved it away to the east on a hill. I always kept Duncan's other beacon in sight. At last, seeing the light coming toward me rewarded me. Duncan had picked it up and was now making for what he thought was the wagon. When he got near me, he had to go down through a small gully, and when he was out of sight I blew out the light. When he came out of the gully, there was not any light in sight and the fun began. As he had a light with him, I had no trouble keeping him in sight. He milled around like a lost sheep, getting farther and farther away from his wagon. He was jabbering in Gaelic all the time. From the tone of his voice, he must have been cussing, but I may have been wrong for he might have been praying. Gaelic always sounded to me as if the speaker was cussing. I got tired of following him and decided to give him one big scare and then take him to his wagon. I crept as near as I dared without him seeing me in the lantern light. I took off my coat, bundled it up, rammed it into my hat, and then threw it at him. It hit him in the back. He let one scream out, dropped his lantern, and took to his heels. He did not go very far until he fell down a gully. I came to his rescue. He was sobbing like a baby and trembling like a leaf. I picked up the lantern, and by its light, he soon recognized me. I thought at first that he would be mad, but no, he was so tickled to see me that he could hardly speak. I felt rather ashamed, as I knew that I had carried the joke too far. I did not realize that anyone could be so afraid of the dark.

The next summer [1908], I got a dose of my own medicine. It was a very hot night in July. I had been riding over in the Red Water country, which was about thirty miles from the ranch. On the return trip, I was overtaken by night, and as I had a long stretch of the badland country to cross before reaching the ranch, I made camp, because there was not any ranch nearby where I could spend the night. It was bad country to travel through in the daylight; consequently, I knew that it would be next to an impossibility to cross it at night. I picketed my horse and rolled up in my saddle blanket, with the intention of spending a peaceful night. I spent the night all right, but it was anything but a peaceful one. The night was dark as the proverbial black cat. It also was hot and sultry. I dropped to sleep quickly as I was very tired. I had not been asleep very long when my horse's snorting awakened me. I sat up and listened, and I heard the noise that I dreaded more than any other noise that I have ever heard. Animals as well as man dread the warning of the old sidewinder or rattlesnake. The noise seemed to be between my horse and me. I soon detected more. It seemed to me that I was in a den of rattlesnakes! I could hear them all around, and I was afraid to move and afraid to stand still. I was wishing that I could get to my horse. I would have spent the rest of the night on his back. To move from my position would have been dangerous. Finally, I stood up and wrapped the saddle blanket around my legs. I had on high leather boots and chaps, so in addition with the blanket, I knew I was as well protected as I could be.

Photo permission given by Lynne Hadley & Jack McRae
L & L Hadley <amitie@bigpond.com>
jmcrae@midrivers.com

Milroy Ranch looking at Spring Creek

During the latter part of July and the first of August, the snakes shed their skins, and they are in a very bad humor during this time. They will strike at anything that comes within their reach. Daylight was the one thing that I longed for most of all. I dared not take a step, and what was I to do? I did not know. It was about five hours until daylight, and I did not want to stand still that long. However, standing still was the only thing that I could do. As the saying goes, "When in doubt have another drink," but as I had nothing to drink I made a smoke. As I lighted my cigarette, the flame of the match gave me an idea. If I had a fire, I would be able to see and then I would be all right. I dropped the lighted match into the grass to see if the grass would burn. The match went out before the grass caught fire. I had an old letter in my pocket. With another match I lighted the letter and tossed it away from me into the grass. Now I had better luck. The grass caught and it was not long before I had a small prairie fire going. Thank goodness, there was no wind. The fire burned a circle into which I quickly moved, taking my saddle and other things with me. I could see what I was doing, and I could see my horse. I let the fire burn close enough to him for me to get hold of the picket rope. I beat out a part of the fire and led the horse into the circle. I am sure that the horse realized what was wrong as he rubbed his nose against me to show that he was glad to have my company. He was not afraid of the fire. Whether the fire burned the snakes, I do not know or care. It kept burning, and all that I did was keep it under control, which was not hard to do, as the grass was not very thick. After what seemed a century to me, morning came and as soon as it was light enough to see, I started for the ranch. I did not get home until noon and I did not tell about my dreadful experience.

I stayed four years on the ranch and in the nearby country. As I now look back and think of the many happy days I spent there, I wonder just why I left. The cold winters and hot dry summers, and the beautiful days between when I would explore the badlands, are but a fond memory now. Out in the badlands I found a very fine spring of water, where there was not supposed to be any water for miles. I built a shack near the spring and there trapped coyotes and bobcats. I also had many a good meal from the sage hens. Those happy days spent in Montana by a carefree reckless youth are gone forever.

Photo taken by William L. Bakewell and placed on postcards. (1909) Note the skins hanging from the roofline and William in middle of picture.

Bakewell's Montana Trapping Shack

Why I ever left that country is a mystery to me, but I now suppose it to be the same evil spirit that caused me to leave a good home seven or eight years before. Why we cannot be satisfied when we are well off is a question no man has yet answered. I would get the call to go and go I did. This was the longest that I stayed in any place during my rambles.

During the winter of 1910, three of us, Sam Sherman, Charlie Hinkle, and I were trapping along the Missouri River southeast of Glasgow, Montana. One morning the sheriff and a posse rode up to our shack. They were looking for a man named Jewels. He was wanted for the killing of the sheriff of Sweet Grass County. They did not find him in that part of the country, but he was caught elsewhere.

It was through the preceding incident that I first heard of an outlaw that I should mention now and later. For several days after the sheriff's visit, we talked a great deal about outlaws, and it was in one of these conversations that I first heard of an outlaw whom I shall call Red. His real name I will not reveal. I know that there are many in the west and others who will remember him by the following narrative.

Back around the year 1905 in the northern part of Montana, a small rancher's son was accused of killing a calf that belonged to one of the large cattle companies. He was arrested and put in jail. He claimed that he was innocent, but he was tried and convicted. He escaped jail and some say he went to Canada. But did he? I will let the reader decide that question.

One night I stopped at Lismas, Montana, where a ferry crossed the Missouri River. In the bunkhouse there were three other men, one of whom I did not know. From one of the men that I knew, I learned that the stranger was a brother of Red, and they resembled each other very much.

During the next two years, I drifted around Montana, Idaho, and Nevada. In my rambles I often heard of an outlaw who was wanted very much. There was a price on his head and his description always answered Red's. In November of 1913, I landed in the town of Gerlach, Nevada. I was cold, tired, and hungry. I put my horse in a livery barn and went to look for something to eat, which I soon found at Scott Butler's. He was the town marshal and proprietor of the two saloons which the town boasted. I ordered a drink for the house, which consisted of Scott Butler and a fellow sitting behind the stove on the wood box. I thought that I had seen the stranger before but as I could not remember where, I did not say anything until I was sure.

Our conversation was on the weather and things pertaining to the country in general. I remarked that it seemed no matter where I went, I always hit a lot of cold weather, and I believed Nevada was as cold as Montana. As I mentioned Montana, my new acquaintance from the wood box asked me how long I had spent in Montana. I told him about five years. He then wanted to know what part, and I said from the Yellowstone north to the line. His face gave a twitch as he said that he had worked there at one time. "How are things there now?" he inquired. I replied that they were fine and that I wished I were there. Before we had finished three or four rounds of drinks, we discovered that there were many things in Montana that were familiar to both. I soon decided that I had met his brother in the person of the stranger in the bunkhouse at Lismas, Montana, but I did not say anything at that time. We had supper together at a Chinese Restaurant, I paid the bill as my new acquaintance was broke, and I saw that he was downhearted, sore at the world in general, and that the best thing in the U.S.A. was the shortest way out.

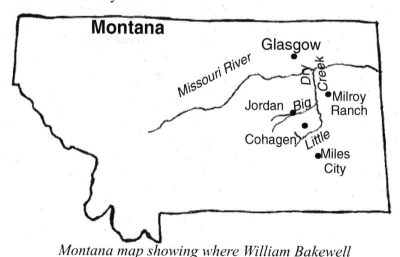

Montana map showing where William Bakewell worked and trapped.

Map by Elizabeth Rajala—2004

45

I stayed around Gerlach a few days and sold my outfit as I was bound for the coast, and I thought a Western Pacific train would be more comfortable to ride than a horse. I was right for once in my life as there was plenty of snow in the Sierras.

Before I left I slipped Red a piece of change and wished him luck, saying that maybe we would meet again. "Well if we do," Red replied, "I hope that I have money, and you are broke so that I can show you how I appreciate what you have done." As we shook hands before I got on my train, I whispered a few words and gave his hand a squeeze. His face flushed, "You are right," he said, "Are they all well?" I nodded as he said thanks and goodbye. I steamed out of Gerlach, little thinking that I should ever see Red again. But this is a small old ball of mud after all.

My first daylight view of California was at Portola the next morning. The snow was very deep, and it was colder than Billie be damn. I guess that if I went to Hades, they would have a spell of cold weather. After thirty minutes for ham and the works, the train dropped down Feather River canyon into a warmer climate, and eventually we reached Sacramento in the afternoon. That night I caught a river boat to San Francisco, which welcomed me with a cold drizzling rain, so I felt perfectly at home.

My sojourn in California did not last very long as my financial resources were soon at low tide.

Chapter 4
Time at Sea

End of 1913 – Beginning of 1914

I chummed with a young Scotsman who was about in the same financial standing as me. He had been out of work for sometime and had decided to go back to sea. He was a sailor but had been working ashore. He wanted me to go with him, which I very readily consented to do. Work was very scarce at that time, and as I had always had a longing to go to sea, this was my chance. We were in luck. A British full rig, three-masted ship, called the *Philadelphia*[6], was signing on a crew. It was bound for Europe, and I signed on as an "able seaman." Some nerve, as all my sea going experience was a few weeks on the lakes. But I was pretty handy with a rope and good at climbing, so I made out all right.

A tug towed us outside of the Golden Gate Bridge and with what appeared to me a lot of hustle and confusion we got the sails set. I heard the captain say to the mate, that it was one of the best jobs of setting sails that he had had for a long time; besides he had a good crew. I found out afterwards that this was true. The crew was made up of many nationalities, French, Norwegian, Finnish, Dutch, American, and also Scots.

There were eighteen men before the mast; this gave nine men to each watch. I was on the port watch. The first mate is in charge of the port watch and the second mate is in charge of the starboard watch. The captain does not stand a watch, but in bad weather, he is on deck, or in the chart room where he can keep an eye on things and see how the ship is being handled.

---

[6] The *Philadelphia* left San Francisco on January 20, 1914.

Both mates were very young. The first mate was only twenty-two and the second mate was a year or two younger. The captain of a sailing ship has a big responsibility. He must be always on the alert for sudden changes in the weather, and must be able to make quick decisions. If he is a few minutes too slow in giving the order to shorten sail, it may mean the loss of some of his sails or the masts, and possibly the ship and all hands. I am very happy to say that very able officers man the British ships and the *Philadelphia* was no exception.

We did not have any bad weather to speak of on our run down to Cape Horn. We were becalmed in the doldrums north of the equator for a few days. It was there that I had my first sample of a captain's wrath. One of the Dutch sailors, by the name of Bill Van Dyke, and I took a swim. The ship was not making any headway, and the sea was as smooth as glass; the weather was as hot as Hades. It was our watch below on the first dogwatch[7], so the two Bills took a dive off the fo'c'sle head and swam to the fore rigging where we had a rope hanging over the side to climb aboard with. It was after the third or fourth dive that the captain spied us. He let out a roar like a Comanche Indian on the warpath. "What in the hell and damnation are you two *!#*& fools trying to do, drown yourselves or make bait for the sharks? A nice mess you two are trying to get me into. A nice report I would have to give to the Board of Trade. Two men lost at sea while bathing. A hell of a master of a ship that can't keep his men aboard his ship while at sea. Say, what do you think this is – a bathing beach? Let's have no more of this or you will get what you both deserve." Whatever that was to be, I have no idea; nonetheless, I know that Bill Van Dyke and I took no more swims.

We had one sailor, a Scotsman by the name of Campbell, who was what the sailors call moon crazy. When the moon was full, he would walk the deck talking to himself, cursing, and swinging his hands about. He was a very disagreeable

---

[7]4-6 pm or 6-8 pm.

fellow at his best. None of the sailors liked him, not even his own countrymen—and there were three other Scotsmen on board. Campbell and I had had words several times. He did not have any use for Americans and was everlasting throwing slurs at me. As a rule, I did not pay any attention to him, as I knew he was only half-baked at the most. One day he went a little too far, and I let him have it on the nose. He weighed about one hundred eighty-five pounds, while I tipped the scales at one hundred twenty-five. At first, I thought I would get the worst of it, but I was mad and didn't care. It took me only a minute to find out that Campbell couldn't fight. In the first place, he was too muscle-bound, and second, he had no heart. A couple of punches in the face took all the fight out of him. The fight was over before it hardly begun and for my part forgotten but not so with Campbell. A few nights after the fight, Campbell, a little German ordinary seaman, and I were aloft taking in a sail. I set down on the footrope to pass the gasket[8] around the sail. Campbell tried to knock me off, and I am afraid if it had not been for the little German, he would have succeeded. The German took his sheath knife and gave Campbell a jab in the ribs which quickly stopped him. As soon as we were on deck, I went for him but the mate stopped me before I could get working on him with the belaying pin that I had grabbed. The German told the mate what the trouble was. The mate said, "He deserves a good dose of the belaying pin soup, and I wish I could let you give it to him but I can't. The captain will take care of him." The captain demoted him to an ordinary seaman and put him in the second mate's watch. If there was any dirty or disagreeable work to do, the second mate saw that Campbell did it. From then on, the rest of the crew made life miserable for him. Campbell stayed clear of me as I

---

[8] Lightlines for securing a furled sail to a boom, gaff or yard.

49

told him I would beat his head off if he bothered me again. I kept a weathered eye on him as I did not know what he might try to do, but I had no more trouble. The captain made the German a seaman.

Credit: "Sea Breezes" June 1953, No. 90, Vol. 15 (New Series)
Permission: Steve Robinson, Senior Administrator—Sea Breezes, Isle of Man

The Golden Gate hit the breakwater at Montevideo—
October 1914. Bakewell was discharged October 13, 1914

We made a good run to the south, and on the first of April [1914], we were off Cape Horn. The weather was clear and cold. I gazed to the South and wondered what there was in that part of the world. Little did I think that before many years I was to know. I do not like cold weather, but it seems that I am forever letting myself be drawn to cold countries. We made a fine run around the Horn and did not hit any bad weather until we were off the Falkland Islands. The weather then made up for the past, present, and future. Blow, yes, and then some. We were hove to under fore and main lower topsails for three days with the decks awash the whole time. The captain claimed that it was the worst blow that he had ever experienced in his forty-five years at sea. As I now look back at the eight years that I spent at sea, it was the worst that I ran into. But bad weather is like a sailor's payday: it doesn't last forever. We were soon sailing into warmer weather, the tropics, the line, and the doldrums. A little bad weather in the Bay of Biscay and then we sailed into quaint old Falmouth for orders.

First time at sea—Philadelphia. Left San Francisco on Janary 20, 1914. Notice that Canada is given as place of birth.

Our orders were for Dublin, Ireland. We were given our pay in Dublin. I received nineteen pounds, ten shillings for the five months and eighteen days work, all in gold. Less than a hundred dollars and it only lasted me part of a month, but I had a good time.

Dublin was not a good port for a sailor to ship out of unless he had plenty of discharge papers, but I was lucky again as I got a chance to make a run to Cardiff, Wales, with a Norwegian four mast Bark, called the *Thistle Bank*. I received thirty shillings for this run, which was not bad for those times.

I was not in Cardiff but a few days when I heard about a four mast Bark in Newport called the *Golden Gate*. As it was signing on a crew, I managed to get my name on the Articles. She was bound for Montevideo loaded with coal. We had a very different crew than that on the *Philadelphia*, as it consisted mostly of boys, apprentices, ordinary seamen, and a very few of the able seamen with any sailing ship experience. The captain was a Nova Scotian who had the name of being a hard case, but I did not find him such. He liked his drink and as a rule was about two sheets to the wind, but he was all right with the crew. The food was very much better than it was on the *Philadelphia*.

With good weather, baring a few squalls, it was but a short run to the River Plata, and we sailed right up to the roadstead off Montevideo. The captain would not take a pilot. He said that he new Montevideo better than the pilot did. We dropped anchor in the roads. It was late in the day and as all hands had been on deck since early morning, we were dead tired and were surely glad to hear the mate order all hands below. He put an old sailor (a man in his sixties) on anchor watch. We got our supper and soon turned in for what we thought would be an all-night sleep, but if there is one place in this world where you can get fooled, it is on a sailing ship. Before daylight we were awakened with, "All hands on deck, we are dragging the anchor and drifting on to the breakwaters." This was very true and not at all pleasant.

A black sou'wester had come up during the night and as the pilot had said, we were in poor anchorage, but the captain had said that he knew what he was doing. Perhaps he did.

The wind was sure blowing and through the rain and spray, we could see the breakwaters but a short way to the leeward. There was nothing we could do but wait, as both anchors were set. We did not have long to wait until we were aground astern, and very soon, our bow was up against the breakwater. The ship took a sharp list to port but did not pound much which was a good thing for us, or she would soon have gone to pieces. The sea was breaking over us and we could not stay on deck. We were all under the fo'c'slehead or in the fo'c'sle. It continued to blow that day and night. The next morning the wind had died down but a heavy sea was running. Two boats came out and managed to get a line fast to us, but they could not do anything. In a few days, we were having fine weather, and lighters were brought along side to salvage the coal.

The first news that we had of the war[9] was from the pilot; it was very brief, and we were all very much excited and anxious for more news. We were glad to get the newspapers that the small boats brought out to us as soon as they could come along side.

We were anxious to get our pay and get ashore, but it was several days before we did. Our plans were to get a ship to Europe as soon as possible, and as Montevideo was a poor place to get a ship, two young Welshmen[10] and I went to Buenos Aires by riverboat. A night's run and we were in Buenos Aires. Buenos Aires is a very fine city and a great port, with modern docks and ships from all parts of the world. As our pay was very small, we looked for work immediately. There were a great many ships in port and plenty

---

[9] World War I.

[10] One of the shipmates was Perce Blackborow, who was soon to be the stowaway on the *Endurance*.

of sailors who had been working ashore. They were coming back for the higher wages and with the Norwegian and other foreign sailors off the interned German ships, there were plenty of men for the demand at that time. Wages on board the ships had gone up. As all ships that could be made sea worthy were being repaired and fitted up to take cargo to Europe, the supply of men would not last long.

I intended to get a ship to England, but I guess my destiny was in another direction. While wandering around the docks, I spied a three-mast auxiliary Barquentine, and I said to one of my shipmates, "There is the ship that I am going to sail on, she sure looks good to me."[11] This was said in an idle jest, but it turned out to be a fact.

After getting along side I saw the name on her stern, *Endurance*, London.[12] Upon closer view she did not look so neat and trim, as the deck was littered with boxes and crates of all shapes and sizes and at least a thousand dogs. However, gaining better information, I found there were only sixty-three, but just the same that was a great amount of dogs. I knew that the dogs were Canadian Huskies. I started a conversation with the quartermaster on the gangway who was a Scotsman. He informed me that they were bound for the Antarctic and that there was an opening for one sailor. He told me to go aboard and see the mate, if I cared to, but that they had turned down a number of men already; perhaps I would have better luck.

Immediately, I took advantage of his suggestion, and was soon being interviewed by the mate. The first questions asked me were if I had had any sailing ship experience, also what kind of ships, and what was the last ship. I replied that I had had sailing ship experience on a square-rigged ship and had just been paid off the *Golden Gate*, which was

---

[11] Bakewell also used to say that it was love at first sight.

[12] The *Endurance* was a wooden ship, 144 feet in length with a 25-foot beam. In addition to its sails, it had a 350 horsepower, coal-fired steam engine. The ship was built at the Framnaes shipyard in Sandefjord, Norway at a cost of $67,000.

on the breakwaters at Montevideo. "Oh! So you were one of the crew of the *Golden Gate*; we saw her as we stopped at Montevideo on our way up the river," he said. I knew that I had the mate interested and that I could get by him O.K. When the Commander, Sir Ernest Shackleton, came into the mate's cabin, the mate said, "I have a sailor here with experience in sail." Sir Ernest asked me where I came from. I told him and he then wanted to know what work I had done ashore. I told him lumberjack, teamster on a grading outfit through western Canada, cowpuncher, ranch hand, trapper, and on the bum between times.[13] He said, "You are the man we want if you can pass the doctors."

Once more luck was with me. I passed the doctors O.K. and one doctor passed a nice big bottle and a glass to me. It was not near beer or lemon squash either. I could see right away that I was going to like the ship. I was to get ten pounds[14] per month and a bonus, all clothes, tobacco, and everything that was needed. My last ship only paid four pounds and ten shillings and no outfit, some difference.

I was given a suit of Navy ducks and blue uniform. The mate asked me to turn to [get to work] right away, as there would be more stores coming aboard and that I could sign on in a day or two. That was O.K. with me, and that is the way I became a member of the British Trans Antarctic Expedition, Sir Ernest Shackleton, Commander.[15]

[13] Bakewell told Sir Ernest he was a Canadian and no one knew any different until the fiftieth reunion of the expedition that was held in London in 1964.
[14] Some books say 8 pounds
[15] Bakewell also told his family that Shackleton impressed upon him that the chance of safe return could be doubtful. Bakewell's reply was that he wasn't concerned about it. That whatever comes happens.

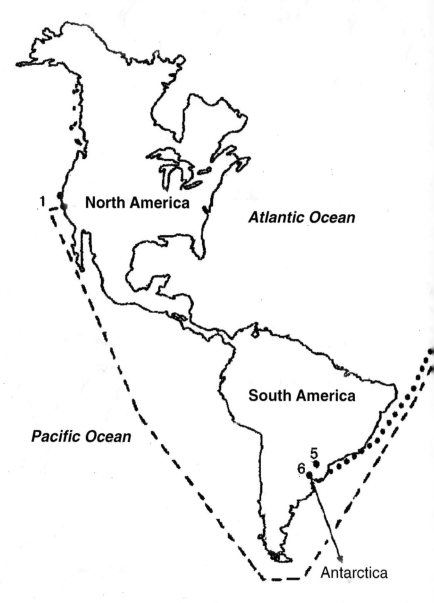

William Bakewell Takes to Sea

North America

Atlantic Ocean

Pacific Ocean

South America

Antarctica

Map made by Mary Rajala Severson—2004

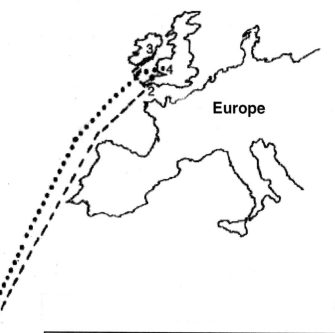

Europe

Legend:

— — —	San Francisco, California USA—The *Philadelphia* set sail January 20, 1914
1	The *Philadelphia Route*
2	Falmouth, England for orders
3	Dublin, Ireland—ship unloaded
4	Newport, Wales
• • •	The *Golden Gate* set sail summer of 1914. This was the first flagship through the new locks.
5	Montevideo—hit breakwater
6	Buenas Aires—joined the *Endurance* for Antarctic Expedition

Chapter 5
The *Endurance*

Little did I think on that day in April while off Cape Horn that I would ever get the chance to see that part of the world south of the Horn; now seven months had hardly passed and I was on my way.

On October 26, 1914, we sailed from Buenos Aires. We were given a big sendoff, whistles blowing, ships with their flags flying, crowds cheering, and the band on the *Argentine Man O' War,* which escorted us out of port playing, "It's A Long Way to Tipperary." Before we returned, I am sure that Tipperary would have been a much more desirable place than where we were at times.

On our second day out of Buenos Aires, one of the sailors went to a locker for some clothing. As he reached in, something moved and he came yelling on deck. Upon investigation, we found a stowaway much to my surprise, he was one of my shipmates on the *Golden Gate*.[16]

From Buenos Aires, we had good weather to the Island of South Georgia which was inhabited by Norwegian whalers. There were four or five whaling stations on the island. I was in two of the stations, and they were very

---

[16] William Bakewell and Walter How had been responsible for hiding the stowaway. Of course, they never admitted to the crime. The stowaway, Perce Blackborow, had tried to sign onto the ship but he was not yet twenty-one. Blackborow became the steward although it has been said that Sir Ernest had told him that if the crew got hungry he would be the first to be eaten! Although later, they were near starvation, this never happened. Bakewell, How, and Blackborow remained close friends until their dying days and their families remain friends to this day.

This photograph is reproduced with the permission of the Scott Polar
Research Institute
Photo by Frank Hurley

Stowaway—Perce Blackborow

He was too young to sign up on the "Endur-
ance." How and Bakewell stowed him away.

<u>Note</u>: Mrs. Chippy, Henry McNish's male tabby cat was
a shipboard favorite. He is shown perched on the shoulder
of Perce Blackborow. From *Endurance:* Shackleton's
Legendary Antarctic Expedition, an exhibit at the
American Museum of Natural History in New York City
recording the twenty-month ordeal from August 1914 to
October 1916.

The Endurance
Expedition Route
1914—1916

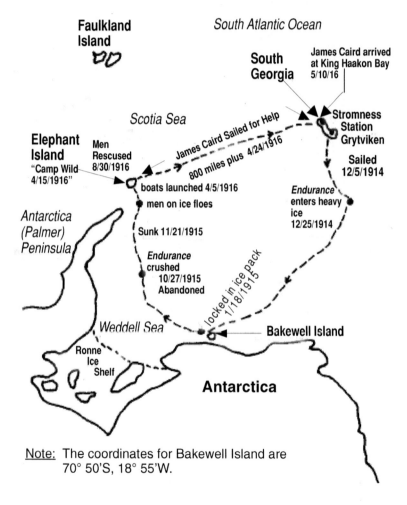

Faulkland Island

South Atlantic Ocean

South Georgia

James Caird arrived at King Haakon Bay 5/10/16

Scotia Sea

James Caird Sailed for Help

Stromness Station Grytviken

Elephant Island
"Camp Wild 4/15/1916"

Men Rescued 8/30/1916

800 miles plus 4/24/1916

boats launched 4/5/1916

Sailed 12/5/1914

men on ice floes

Endurance enters heavy ice 12/25/1914

Antarctica (Palmer) Peninsula

Sunk 11/21/1915

Endurance crushed 10/27/1915 Abandoned

locked in ice pack 1/18/1915

Weddell Sea

Bakewell Island

Ronne Ice Shelf

Antarctica

Note: The coordinates for Bakewell Island are 70° 50'S, 18° 55'W.

(Map by Jim Carter—from National Geographic and other sources)
Permission given to Elizabeth Bakewell Rajala to print.

much alike. There was a factory where the whale blubber was rendered into oil, bunkhouses for the men, mud, and an exceedingly strong odor of whale.[17]

At Grytviken, where we stayed most of the time, there was an old graveyard[18] and in it were buried some American whalers. The rough markers showed that some were buried in the early part of the eighteenth century. One I remember was from New Bedford, Massachusetts. I do not remember any of their names but it was very fascinating to me, and I made several visits there during our stay. I often thought what a surprise it would be to the old time whalers if they could come back to life and see how they catch whales now. Harpoons are shot from a gun with an explosive in the points to stun the whales. The old timers had to use hand harpoons and then probably battled for hours before they could finish the whale with a lance. Now whalers use fast steam tugs and the old timers had to use sail or rowboats. The men at South Georgia were mostly from the northern part of Norway, fine big men, very skillful in their work, and very agreeable. They took a great interest in the Expedition and always wanted to help us or give us something. After a month's stay, we left and it was with many sad regrets that we parted from our new friends. It was the last that we were to see of civilization for a long time. It would be much longer than we expected, as we intended to be back to spend the winter in South Georgia. It did not turn out that way. On the morning of December 5th, we started down the coast on a southeasterly course. Before long, South Georgia was nothing but a blur on the horizon and one more place in our memories.

---

[17] Whaling has long been gone from South Georgia due to the depletion of the whales and seals. Slowly their population is increasing, but no whaling stations are in operation today. Grytviken is the capital of South Georgia. Besides the empty, rusting whaling buildings and equipment, there is a delightful little museum and a renovated Norwegian church. One family currently lives at Grytviken, Tim and Pauline Carr. Nearby at King Edward Point is a small British military garrison because it is an U.K. dependent territory. The other whaling stations on South Georgia are in further decay.

[18] This whaler's cemetery still exists and is the resting place for Sir Earnest Shackleton.

Our ship was a queer sight with the extra coal that we had loaded on deck at South Georgia. Also, over sixty dogs, whale meat hanging in the rigging (for the dogs), stores, and I don't know what all on deck, made us look anything but a trim ship. To help matters along, we had a cat and whenever the dogs would get sight of her, you would have thought that all bedlam had broken loose. She was a very smart cat and knew enough to keep out of the way of the dogs. If she had not, it would have been goodbye cat.[19] The dogs were very savage and were always on the look out for a fight or whatever trouble they could get into.

We were one of the best-equipped expeditions that ever went south. There was everything in the line of food and clothing for our comfort and everyone seemed happy.[20]

The Sandwich Islands were the next land we passed coming out of South Georgia. They are small and rocky, uninhabited islands. We sighted many icebergs and had to keep a sharp look out for large lumps of ice or growlers, as they are much larger than they appear to be. To run the ship into one might cause severe damage. It was at the southern part of the Sandwich Islands that we ran into the first pack ice. A heavy swell was running and Sir Ernest was very anxious about how the ship would tolerate the ice. The ship was new and had been built of the best materials for withstanding ice. However, as that was the first ice we had encountered, it was only natural that Sir Ernest would feel anxious until he could see what she would do. The *Endurance*

---

[19] The cat, Mrs. Chippy, belonged to the carpenter, Mr. McNish, and he was very fond of her. Mrs. Chippy provided a great deal of entertainment for the men, and became a good friend of Blackborow's. When the men ended up on the ice, she had to be sent to "kitty heaven." Mr. McNish was very upset about this drastic action and never forgot. Two more interesting facts about the cat: she dearly loved to tease the dogs, and she was a tomcat.

[20] Of particular interest to Bakewell was the well-stocked library. During his time onboard, he claimed to have read every book more than once. He also said that Shackleton would ask How and him many questions and their opinions of the books.

lived up to her name. She rammed and wormed her way through the ice. We continued through or around pack ice for many days. The young ice did not present any difficulty. The old ice was too thick to break through so we had to go around. There were many open leads or lanes in the ice. Here we could make good time. In the open water, we saw many seals, penguins, and whales of different kinds. The killer whale attracted the most attention. He is just a large species of the shark[21] and eats seals, penguins, and would not object to a sailor if one should drop into his way. Therefore, he was held in awe and disdain.

The penguins were a source of great amusement. When Clark, one of the scientists, was at the wheel they would run along on the ice as fast as they could, calling "clark, clark, clark" and they seemed quite indignant at him for not stopping the ship and waiting for them. Another funny incident with the penguins happened one afternoon when some of them came near the ship while Hussey, the meteorologist, was playing Tipperary on his banjo. They seemed to like the music very much, but when he changed to some Scottish Aires, they fled, and the noise of the laughter from the men scared them so that they ran just as fast as they could.

The routine was very much the same from day to day. Fighting our way through the pack ice, taking every advantage of any leads or young ice was a challenge. At times we were fast for hours and had to wait patiently for the pack to open.

Christmas Day [1914] we had a big celebration. Many good things to eat, plenty of grog, and Hussey, one of the scientists, entertained us with some fine music on his banjo and a one-string violin. The wind was so strong that we could not make any headway so we did nothing but enjoy ourselves.

---

[21] A mistaken belief held at that time.

The time between Christmas and New Year's was uneventful. Some days we made ten to fifteen miles and other days a little better and some less. After the New Year, we had better conditions. The ice became looser, and we had some large leads of open water. There were bergs in sight all the time, and at times when the sun was shining on them, they were very beautiful. They were of many different shapes and we could see the likeness of ships, castles, and many other things. All their beauty was spoiled in knowing that they were just ice. As we could not see anything but ice most of the time, we would have appreciated the sight of a ship or something that was not ice.

Painting comissioned by Elizabeth Bakewell Rajala from Walter E. How, a close friend of William Lincoln Bakewell.

Endurance and More Ice

Wherever there was any open water, it was teaming with life. Schools of whales, penguins, and seals were all around us. They apparently made that part of the world their home in summer; they are welcome to it, as I have seen places that are more desirable.

We had been on the lookout for land as the water had become shallower and a previous expedition had found that land was in sight. I have very good eyesight, but darned if I could see anything that looked like land. At that instant, one of the dogs got his chain wrapped around my leg. Immediately, I thought that land, yes, that is the place for dogs rather than on board a ship. I spied something in the distance that sloped from the sea to a height of eight or ten hundred feet. As we came closer, we could see that it was a very rolling country; however, no rocks or earth were visible, just snow and ice and all a dull gray color. It had anything but an inviting appearance, and in most places, the barrier ice was higher than the ship's mast.[22] There were very few places where it would have been possible to make a landing. We sailed to the south, keeping the land in sight. At times, we would have open water and then more forcing through the pack. It was very slow work. Sir Ernest was trying to get to Vahsel Bay, which a German expedition had reached, but we were out of luck. On or around the 20th of January 1915,[23] we became fast in the ice and although we made many attempts to get out, they were of no avail. We were frozen in for the winter. Our destination was S 79° 20', W 35° or farther south if we could have made it, but the nearest we ever reached was S 79° about twenty miles from where we wanted to go.

Sir Ernest intended to land a shore party there, and he and some of the men (or all if it was advisable), were going to make the journey across the Antarctic Continent to the Ross Sea, where another expedition would meet him. The Ross Sea party was to have laid out depots for Sir Ernest and his party, but this overland journey was not to be.

As soon as we saw there was not any chance of getting the ship out of the ice, and as nothing could be done until next summer, we began to prepare for the winter. All the dogs were landed on the ice. That was a great relief as we could walk about the

---

[22] The uninviting land they saw was Coats Land on mainland Antarctica.
[23] Most sources give January 18, 1915 as the day they became beset in the ice.

deck without the danger of having an arm or leg snapped off. The dogs liked the ice as they could get more exercise, although they were kept tied. We gathered in all the seals and penguins that we could get for food for the dogs and ourselves. One of the lady dogs presented us with four fine pups. As the pups were allowed to run free, they furnished a variety of amusements for us. They were like big balls of fluff and were always into no end of mischief.

The dog drivers started to train teams and it sure was some fun. Each dog seemed to have a grudge against all the other dogs and all they wanted to do was fight. Until each dog became acquainted with his mates and learned which dog was the leader, it was one royal battle. After the teams stopped fighting among themselves, they would fight with the other teams whenever a chance came. One day three teams got together: twenty-one dogs all trying to eat one another at the same time. Tangled harness, dogs, men, sledges, hair, and snow were all in one heap. Oh! What a mess that had to be untangled and repaired for use. We built houses of slabs of ice for the dogs but unless the weather was extremely bad, they slept on top of their houses.[24]

The work[25] was divided very fairly between all the hands so that none of us were overworked and we settled down for the winter. The days were getting shorter and the temperature was going lower each day. We did not mind the cold as we had plenty of warm clothing and an abundance of good food. The long cold winter had no terrors for us. Our living quarters were very comfortable and we had many different things to help pass the time. Dog team races were very popular. Football on the ice was a big novelty. The out-of-doors sports lasted until the sun left us, then cards, checkers, banjo music, and the

---

[24] The men referred to the doghouses and dogiloos.

[25] Bakewell truly respected Shackleton and his method of discipline because Shackleton was very fair and did not believe in unnecessary discipline. Shackleton assigned daily jobs regardless of the person's station in life.

Gramophone[26] furnished our inside amusement.

We had a very large library, containing one of the largest collections of polar books ever gotten together. I read the complete lot and many a pleasant hour I spent with the old explorers in the Arctic and in the precious expeditions in the Antarctic. We very naturally had our arguments, just like any group of men who were thrown together for any length of time. We each had the war ended in a certain way, at a given time, and our reasons for it. These ways and means would change from time to time. Religion got its raking over. Each one's was the best and if the truth were known, I do not think any of us had any. Different ships and shipmates were talked about. In one of our discourses on old shipmates, McLeod and I discovered that one of my shipmates on the *Philadelphia* had been an old mate of his on the New Zealand coast, and I then remembered this shipmate talking of the ships that McLeod and he had been in together. It is funny but when sailors compare notes they nearly always find a ship or shipmate that they both know.

Do not think that we did not have anything to worry and disturb us, because we did. Although the ship was fast in the ice, there were times when we could hear rumbling and grinding noises, and very often hear lumps of ice striking the keel of the ship. This would happen when the wind was from an easterly or westerly direction. The ice pack blowing against the land would cause pressure, which was our greatest worry. We were in fear that the pressure would smash the ship.

We were drifting all the time and to all points of the compass but mostly to the north and west, leaving the newfound land behind and slowly getting closer to Graham Land. Large bergs traveling through the pack and bergs aground were a never-ending worry. If we should have gotten in their path, our ship would have been smashed like matchwood. Therefore, life on an Antarctic Expedition was not all a bed of roses.

---

[26] Gramophone was a trade name for a phonograph.

April 1915 came and the sun left us for the winter. We had twilight for a few weeks and then the long winter night. There wasn't much work that could be done. After each blizzard, we had to shovel the snow off the ship and the dog kennels. We did not get many hard blows but when it did blow it made up for lost time.

Painting comissioned by Elizabeth Bakewell Rajala from
Walter E. How, a close friend of William Lincoln Bakewell.

Endurance left Buenos Aires for Grytviken, South Georgia.
Spent a month there then left for Antarctica by way of
Weddell Sea to Vahsel Bay

All the time we were drifting to the north. On June 22, 1915, midwinter day, we had some twilight and the ice conditions were not so quiet after midwinter. Open leads could be seen in the distance and there were cracks in the flow very near the ship. Pressure ice was being piled up in all directions and all hands knew it would not be long before something would happen. What that something was to be, was the great worry of all. Sledging rations and other essentials were stored handy in case of a hurried leave of the ship.

The last of July the sun returned and was welcomed by all. The long winter night was over and the daylight was a great help to us in the days that were before us. The first of August 1915, the pressure began to attack the ship, but it failed to get a firm grip and for a time, we were still in possession of a strong little ship.

Members of the Imperial Trans-Antarctic Expedition

Sir Ernest Shackleton
  Leader
Frank Wild
  Second-in-Command
Frank Worsley
  Captain
Lionel Greenstreet
  First Officer
Hubert T. Hudson
  Navigator
Thomas Crean
  Second Officer
Alfred Cheetham
  Third Officer
Louis Rickinson
  First Engineer
A. J. Kerr
  Second Engineer
Dr. Alexander H.
Macklin
  Surgeon
Dr. James A. McIlroy
  Surgeon
James M. Wordie
  Geologist
Leonard D. A. Hussey
  Meteorologist
Reginald W. James
  Physicist

Robert S. Clark
  Biologist
James Francis Hurley
  Official Photographer
George E. Marston
  Official Artist
Thomas H. Orde-Lees
  Motor Expert (later storekeeper)
Harry McNish*
  Carpenter
Charles J. Green
  Cook
William Bakewell
  Able Seaman
Walter How
  Able Seaman
Timothy McCarthy
  Able Seaman
Thomas McLeod
  Able Seaman
John Vincent
  Able Seaman
Ernest Holness
  Fireman
William Stevenson
  Fireman
Perce Blackborow**
  Stowaway (later steward)

*McNish name is spelled a number of ways (Macnish, MacNeish, McNish) but birth certificate is McNish.
**Blackborow has a number of spelling and we have used the family spelling (Blackborro, Blackborrow, and Blackborow)

Photo taken by Frank Hurley and permission to print given by Scott Polar Research Institute.

Early picture taken on the Endurance with some of the crew.

1	Harry McNish	13	Hubert Hudson
2	Ernest Holness	14	Louis Rickinson
3	William Bakewell	15	Walter How
4	Alfred Cheetham	16	Charles Green
5	Thomas Crean	17	James Hurley
6	Leonard Hussey	18	Sir D. Gooch
7	Lionel Geenstreet	19	Robert Clark
8	Reginald James	20	James Wordie
9	Ernest Shackleton	21	Dr. Alexander Macklin
10	Frank Wild	22	George Marston
11	Frank Worsley	23	Dr. James McIlroy
12	William Stevenson		

Chapter 6
Life on the Ice

I do not know of anything that man could construct that would stand the tremendous pressure of millions of tons of ice, if once caught fairly in its grip. Very anxious and busy days followed. All the dogs were brought aboard as the pressure had wrecked their kennels. They were glad to get aboard. They knew something was wrong and they did not offer to fight with one another after being brought on board. As for myself, I could feel that there was going to be a great big adventure for me. I remember one day of saying to myself, "Bill you sure have gotten yourself into one hell of a place." Hell was right.

The first of August 1915, the pressure attacked the ship again and that time we did not escape so easily, as our stern post and rudder were damaged. From then until the 26th of August, (almost a year since I had joined the ship) we did not have any more trouble. On the 26th, the ice started to move again, and good size leads appeared around the ship. Although there were groaning and snapping sounds in the timbers, our good little ship still held together, but we had some anxious moments. On the 2nd of September, I had one of the most startling moments of my life. I was lying in my bunk, when without anymore warning than the usual movement of the ice, which we had had for days; the ship literally jumped into the air and settled on its beam. I also made a record move, being up and out on deck in a split second, wondering what the next move would be. The pressure had lifted us right out of the ice and we were over on our port beam, with heavy pressure working all around us. It looked as if the pressure would force the ice right over the ship but it did not. Our time had not yet come. The pressure eased up some after a time and the ship righted herself some but never on a level keel again. We were given a rest until the last of September; however, around us the pack was never still. The big floe where we had played football and exercised the dogs was broken up and pressure ice was piled all around, making it a very different place.

The dogs sensed the danger and would at times howl just like the wolves that I had heard so often in good old Canada. How I wished I were then in Canada, as you can probably guess.

The dogs were not the only ones that were affected. There was a silent and serious look on every face as all realized that the critical moment was not far off. After many days of anxiety, the fatal day came on October 27, 1915. Our poor little ship had to give up the battle. The pressure attacked her on all sides. She had made a game fight but the ice was the stronger.

All hands were ordered to leave the ship. We took the dogs and the stores that had been in readiness for sometime and placed them at a safe distance from the ship. Our nearest land was Paulet Island, some three hundred and fifty miles west and north. There a Swedish expedition[27] had built a hut and left supplies for any expedition that should meet with distress.

That would be just a nice little walk if you do not mind what you say. Three hundred and fifty miles is a long walk when you have good old Mother Earth under your feet. However, when it is over a mass of broken ice, with pressure ridges ten or twenty feet high to climb over, and when the whole mass may open at any moment and leave you on a floating island of ice, it is another story.

---

[27]The Nordenskjold hut was built on Paulet Island in 1902 by a Swedish expedition. The hut was later stocked with supplies by the Argentine government.

Our first move after leaving the ship was to get the three lifeboats[28] onto a solid floe a short distance from the ship. With dogs, stores, and different equipment that we had taken from the ship, we camped and spent our first night on the ice.

We pitched our tents[29] on what we thought would be a good strong floe, but we had no more than settled for the night when we were called by those on watch and told to get out as the floe was breaking up. There was an opening in the floe through our camp. We had to move everything onto the larger part of the floe. It was anything but a pleasant job to tackle in the dark with the temperature below zero. We finished the night without anymore disturbance from the ice, but we were bothered with the cold. We only had our blankets. Eight of us were in a tent that was made to accommodate four. The crowded condition, though somewhat uncomfortable, enabled us to keep warm. Daylight was most welcome to all, and we were glad to get out of our cramped quarters.

There was a great deal of discouraging work ahead, and the outlook was not very promising. The appearance of everything around us resembled the work of a hurricane. Our ship with its masts all askew, yards and sails hanging every old way but the way they should, was extremely discouraging for us. Stores and other equipment were scattered all over the ice. We were shipwrecked all right but it was one odd looking shipwreck.

We had become very much attached to the ship and beyond our own safety, we felt the loss of the ship more than I can say. Men who follow ships for a living have a feeling for a good ship that is akin to human. Our ship

---

[28] The lifeboats were the *James Caird*, the *Dudley Docker*, and the *Stancomb Wills*. The lifeboats were named after individuals who had provided significant financial support to the expedition.

[29] There were five tents for the 28 men. Bakewell was in tent three along with How, Stephenson, Holness, McCarthy, McLeod, Vincent, and Green.

certainly had been a good one, and now she lay before us shattered, twisted, and torn. It looked as if Father Neptune had poured out all his vengeance upon us for trespassing in his domains.

Painting commissioned by Elizabeth Bakewell Rajala from Walter E. How, a close friend of William Lincoln Bakewell.

Exercising the dogs on the ice when the Endurance was icebound.

After a breakfast of sledging rations and biscuits, we moved all the supplies and gear to a large floe, some three or four hundred yards from the ship. It was called Dump Camp as we dumped everything but what would be necessary for our long journey to land. The junk as we then called it would have brought a fortune in civilization, but there it was just junk. Compasses, chronometers, and other scientific instruments that had been handled so carefully were now thrown around as if we were all on a drunken orgy.

A complete new outfit of clothing was issued to each man and sleeping bags. Right here is where I wish to tell about the only unfair deal that happened on the expedition. There were not enough fur bags for all hands, so some of the wool bags were used to make up the deficiency.

We drew lots to see which kind of a bag each would get. There was some crooked work in the drawing as Sir Ernest, Mr. Wild (second in command), Captain Worsley, and some of the other officers all drew wool bags. The fine warm fur bags all went to the men under them. I think that action was enough to show what wonderful men were in charge. They always took the brunt of things and when there was any danger they were first to go ahead. The safety of his men was Sir Ernest's first thought, his own last.

Painting commissioned by Elizabeth Bakewell Rajala from Walter E. How, a close friend of William Lincoln Bakewell.

Camping on the ice after the Endurance was crushed.

It was wonderful how unconcerned all hands were. Hundreds of miles from any human help, the ship smashed, and food and supplies for three months, the safety of all depended on how the ice behaved.

All around us, the ice floes were grinding each other smaller and smaller. The pressure was piling up ice like long windrows of hay.

We had the three lifeboats on sledges. The boats were very heavy, and the sledges were not made for such heavy loads. It took four sledges under each boat, and then the carpenter had to do a lot of reinforcing. The men were divided into teams for pulling the boats. The dogs were used to pull the sledges loaded with our food, other essentials, and equipment. It was hard work pulling the boats as the ice was so rough in places. A pioneer party had to go in advance and cut a path, and then it was sometimes only with superhuman strength and effort that we were able to get the boats through. The first day we made only about a mile and on the second about another mile. Luckily on the second night we were able to camp on a large floe of old ice.

The next morning the ice around us had opened so much, and so many small leads of open water were in all directions that it was impossible for us to go on with safety until the pack became consolidated again.

We called this camp Ocean Camp. We were in Ocean Camp two months. Between the ship and us, the ice was partly solid. We made many trips to the ship, salvaging what we could in the way of food, tobacco, and clothing. The ice was jammed so tight around the ship that it kept her from sinking. The deck amid ship was under water, but we managed to chop a hole through with long ice chisels. Through the hole, we were able to salvage some cases of canned food. By probing around with a long boat hook, we could get the cases up to the hole, and then they would float to the top. The appearance of each case meant a lot of cheering from the men. Sometimes the cheering would not be so prolonged, especially if the case contained something that was not liked. I remember that one case contained canned spinach, and it did not get a cheer. Although we knew that it was good for us, we were like little boys: we did not like it. On one of these trips to the ship, I got one of the coldest baths that I have ever had. While plundering around the ship, the third officer Crean and I got down into the galley (which was a house on deck). It was half filled with water. We wanted to try to get a big iron pot that was there. The pots we had to cook in were aluminum and we were afraid that they would not last long over the hot blubber fires. The iron pot was in a locker, which was covered with about two feet of water and six or eight inches of ice. We cut a hole in the ice above the door of the locker, but try as we would with a pole, we could not get the door open. I had made up my mind to get that pot. I stripped off my clothes, and Crean held onto my feet, and by going headfirst into the water up to my waist, I opened the door, got the pot, and also some others that were in the locker. There happened to be some cans of salt in that locker too, and we got them. It came in handy as we had not saved a very big supply of salt. Seal meat without salt is not very appetizing. Although the temperature was well below freezing, I did not feel the cold very much, and it took only a few minutes after dressing for me to get warm. As all hands were so enthusiastic over our haul, I felt well paid for my bath.[30]

One day in the latter part of November [21, 1915], while we were lying in our tents, we were startled by the cry, "There she goes." I was out of the tent in quick time to see what was going on. The watchman pointed towards the ship. Her stern was sticking up in the air. The ice had opened and she was going down. Bow first, she dove to her grave in the Briny Deep. There was a queer silence over the camp. As for me, there was an odd lump in my throat, and I found it hard to swallow. I know that many of the others felt the same. Although the ship was a wreck, it still meant much to us. We were now very lonely.

---

[30] On one of the other trips to the ship Bakewell said How and he came by the compartment Hurley used as a dark room. There they saw the cases with the photographic negatives. Wading ankle deep in the water, they retrieved the cases.

We stayed in Ocean Camp until a few days before Christmas, when Sir Ernest decided that the ice was in good condition for us to travel. We were to try to make Paulet Island. We had made considerable drift to the north and Paulet Island was much closer. We were all very anxious to get started.[31]

As there was food that we could not take, we celebrated Christmas a few days ahead of time. We had a large assortment of delicacies that we had salvaged from the ship and as they were not the proper kind of food for a sledging journey, we ate what we could and left the remainder. It was many months before we had our fill of civilized food again.

We started on our march and a harder or more discouraging march I have never had the misfortune to participate in. The dogs hauled the provisions and the men the boats. The boats were the stickers. The dogs could travel right along with their loads but we men with the boats could not make much headway as the ice was so rough. We had to relay the boats. We would take one a short distance and then go back and get the other, this making three trips and causing us to travel several miles in order to advance a mile or so. There was new snow which made the hauling of the boats man killing work. We could have left the boats and made better progress but we would have been in all probability a year in reaching land. The thought of spending a year on the ice was not very pleasant. I heard the carpenter say that if we had to go over much more such rough ice, the boats would not float when we did reach open water. After a week on the trail, we had to give up as the ice ahead was so rough and broken up that further progress was impossible.

---

[31] Bakewell said that Shackleton emphasized the need for taking only the essentials (2# per man), except diaries, banjo, some of Hurley's glass plate negatives, film, and one small camera. Shackleton, himself, tore the 23rd Psalm and Job 38:29-30 from his Bible that Queen Alexandra gave him. He then threw the Bible onto the ice. One of the men (McLeod) picked up the Bible and it is now in the Royal Geographical Society in London.

Once more we made camp. This proved to be our longest and last permanent camp on the sea ice. This camp was called Patience Camp. There our patience was surely given a good try out. We could do nothing but wait, and as the saying goes, "Weight sunk the ship;" however, it did not sink us. We were put to a very severe test in that camp and I am proud to say that we all passed with flying colors.

The food question became very serious. Our sledging rations had to be kept for the boat journey that we would eventually make. We were living on a meat diet and we had trouble getting enough. Twenty-eight men and the fifty-odd dogs remaining could eat more meat than we could at times get. Seals and penguins were very scarce, unless we found open water, and then we did not always find them. We were on very short rations at times, and with our enormous appetites, we were always hungry. Our thoughts and conversations were most of the time on something to eat. The supply of food got so short that we could not afford to feed the dogs any longer. One of the saddest days on the expedition was the day that we had to kill the dogs. We had grown so fond of them, and they were sure good faithful companions.[32] They did more than their share of the work, but they had to be killed, and the camp was a very gloomy place for many days. We avoided going to the side of the floe where they had been put to death. Some of the younger dogs we ate. It was much better meat than either the seal or the penguin, but even so, we did not relish it.

In Patience Camp we stayed nearly three months, and at times, it looked as if we would not drift far enough north to reach open water before another winter. The thought of spending another winter on the ice was discouraging to say

---

[32] Bakewell, who was certainly fond of Sampson, often spoke of the unruliness of the dogs, and saving Mrs. Chippy from becoming dog food was taken in stride.

the least. Our food had become so short that we could not spare much of the blubber to cook with, so our meat was only half cooked. By this time, we did not care whether it was cooked or not. We could eat it raw and had learned to like it. Even the blubber was eaten raw or fried, with a relish. We had become real Eskimos and were only too glad to get meat in any form.

I have read books on how men have risen from savages to become Oxford graduates, but I won't have to write a book to tell how some Oxford graduates sank to the level of savages. All there is to it, is to cut off the food supply and let them get good and hungry. It may take years or even generations for men to reach our state of civilization, but in only a few weeks, they can drop back again.

Around the first of April [1916], we began to see our first signs of land. A seagull flew over us, so we knew that land was not far away. We had drifted too far north for Paulet Island. I now expected that land would be sighted any day and was not disappointed. One morning land was sighted to the west of us. It was Joinville Land. The tall mountain peaks showed up very plain but it was impossible for us to reach the land over the broken ice. Our only hope was for the ice to open, so we could launch the boats. We were drifting very fast to the north and could see black patches of sky farther north and east. Those black patches we knew denoted open water.

Elephant and Clarence Islands lay to the north of us and they were our last hope. If we were carried by them, we would be at the mercy of the South Atlantic, and how long our small boats would last was a question. One morning the air was exceptionally clear, and we sighted Clarence Island. I heard the captain say that it was sixty miles or more away.

Now the most anxious days of our sojourn in the South had come. The ice was moving all around us. We could see the ice move up and down, which we knew was caused by the swell from the open sea. April 19, 1916 fell on Sunday, but it was not a day of rest for us. The ice was scattering out and many of our neighboring floes had broken up into smaller pieces. Our own floe was no better than the others were. Before we had time to realize what was happening, a crack ran across the floe directly through our camp and we had to do some quick work to get our boats, tents, food, and other equipment onto the larger part of the floe. Sir Ernest gave the cook orders to cook all the meat we could eat, as we might have to take to the boats at any moment. For once, we had all that we could eat, after many months of very short rations. Very shortly after we had eaten, the ice opened up with plenty of open water and before I hardly realized what we were doing, we had launched the boats and I was pulling on a fourteen foot oar. Our boat journey had begun.[33]

---

[33] The *James Caird* held Clark, Hurley, Hussey, James, Wordie, McNish, Green Vincent, McCarthy, with Shackleton and Wild in command. Greenstreet, Kerr, Lees, Macklin, Cheetham, Marston, McLeod, and Holness were in the *Dudley Docker* with Worsley in command. The *Stancomb Wills*, which was the smallest and least seaworthy, was commanded by Hudson and Crean. It held the remainder of the crew: Bakewell, How, McIlroy, Rickinson, Stephenson, and Blackborow. Throughout the expedition Bakewell (a small, 125# man) proved his worth and endurance, and showed respect for all. He never even suffered any frostbite effects from the extreme weather conditions.

Chapter 7
Lifeboats Take to Sea

Our first day in the water was one of the coldest and most dangerous of the expedition. The ice was running riot. It was a hard race to keep our boats in the open leads. Wind, current, and tide seemed to all be busy at the same time, and we had many narrow escapes from being crushed when the larger masses of the pack would come together. A couple of hours of hard work got us into more ice-free waters, and for a while our danger was over. We made better progress but just where the leaders were making for, I did not know. I knew that there were several different islands near, as I had heard them spoken of. Where we would be able to get to all depended on the ice, wind, and weather in general.

The first evening we pulled our boats out onto a large floe and camped for the night. We pitched our tents, had supper, and were soon in our sleeping bags. The hard work of the day, after our long idleness, had taken a toll on us. After finishing my good night smoke, I curled up in my bag and was just dropping off into a well-earned sleep, when I was aroused by a terrific noise. The ice had cracked under our tent, in fact under Holness, the sailor who was sleeping next to me. Before we had time to move, the ice opened and Holness dropped into the water. It was only through the quick work of others and me that we were able to get him out. As we pulled him, sleeping bag and all onto the ice, the crack closed. His life was saved by a hair's breadth.

He would have been squeezed to death between hundreds of tons of ice, if we had not been able to reach him.[34] As quickly as we could, we got our outfit together on the larger part of the floe, but there was not anymore sleep that night. We sat huddled around the blubber stove the rest of the night. At daylight, we got under way, starting our second day in the boats. We were cold and tired, but all seemed to be in good spirits.

We found open water to the west of us free from ice, but when we got away from the shelter of the ice, the boats made such heavy weather of it that we had to make back to the ice. Our boats were too heavily loaded to ride a heavy sea. The temperature was around zero and any spray that we would ship, would freeze very quickly. We were suffering badly from the cold, as our clothing was damp or wet. Also the unaccustomed work at the oars was telling greatly on us all.

We camped the second night on a small sloping berg and managed to cook a good feed of sledging rations. The hot food certainly put new life into us. We must have been a queer spectacle moving around on the ice in the light of the blubber stove. I heard whales blowing around us and the thought of the killer whales was always in my mind. They were the one thing that caused me a lot of worry.

We managed to pass the night without our camp being smashed. The night was not all peace and quietness as the berg raised and tossed in the heavy swell of the sea. It also received hard raps from the rest of the ice, but it held together.

---

[34] In another one of Bakewell's writings he recorded this ice incident as follows: "I was sitting up in my sleeping bag having a smoke, when all of a sudden, bang, the ice cracked under Ernest Holness, who was laying in his sleeping bag beside me. He dropped into the crack and I made a grab. Stephenson, who was also sitting up in his sleeping bag on the other side of Holness, made a grab. We were just able to pull him clear when the ice came together. A second later we could not have saved him from being crushed. Sir Ernest then pulled Holness out of the tent. There was a mad scramble to get all our gear together on one piece of the floe. Some how Sir Ernest was left on the deserted piece of floe. We had to launch one of the boats to rescue him. We did not attempt to get any more sleep that night."

On the morning of our third day we were greeted by the sun and a light easterly wind. We were soon on our way. The ice was getting very thin. There were very few pieces left that were large enough to camp on and it looked like we would be forced very soon into the open sea. We headed west with the sails set on all three boats. We were rolling along at a very good rate. We were now headed for a new place, Deception Island. If we could still keep making good time, we (the sailors) figured that we should reach Deception Island that night. At noon, the captain [Worsley] took a shot at the sun and when he figured out the position, we were east of where we had started from in the morning. I am glad the captain was not in the same boat as I was or he probably would have had me keelhauled or hanged at the yardarm, if we had had one. If he had heard the remarks passed by the others and myself, on his ability as a navigator, he would have been justified in hanging us.

The captain was right. A strong current was setting to the east and although we had sailed west, the current had carried us east; therefore it was just another day of disappointment to be added to the many others. The leaders now changed their plans as the circumstances called for, but as these plans were not disclosed, I did not know where we were headed. I surmised they did not want to give us any more disappointments. The weather became colder as night came on and we were all very miserable. We were unable to find a piece of ice large enough to camp on. After a lot of hunting, we found a large lump of ice to which we were able to fasten a rope from one of the boats. We then fastened the second boat behind the first and the third behind the second, each far enough behind the other to ensure safety. In this manner, we started to spend our third night and, "Oh! What a night!" Part of us would huddle up in the bottom of the boat while the others would try to keep the brash ice pushed away from the boat. We often relieved each other so all could get some rest. Pieces of ice were constantly breaking off the piece that we were anchored to. It was hard work to keep the pieces from ramming holes through our boats. We were cold, wet, hungry, thirsty, and disappointed. The night was everything that represented misery, and to make matters worse the drift ice gathered so thick around the large lump to which we were fastened, that we had to cut the painter [line used for securing boats together] loose and get into clear water. We made a sea anchor of our oars by lashing them together. We then lay hove to until daylight. We were suffering greatly from the intense cold. Blackborow, who was our stowaway lad at Buenos Aires, complained of his feet getting numb, and there was not any feeling in them. I tried to get him to keep pounding them together, but he was so all in that I could not get him to do as I suggested. Some of the others were complaining of their fingers. I knew what was wrong: they were freezing, and if we did not get some relief soon or a decided raise in the temperature, our part of the expedition would soon be brought to a close. The temperature was below zero, and with our wet clothing freezing on us and no warm food for two days, we were fast reaching the end of our endurance. I was not bothered by my hands or feet freezing, I was just cold all over.

Daylight came at last. The greatest light in the world. I know it brought a new lease on life for us. The sky was clear and the temperature began to rise. There was a thin skim of ice over the sea but it soon disappeared with the sun. The wind was now fair for us to make Elephant Island.

We had plenty to eat of cold sledging rations but nothing to drink. Our lips were cracked, and our throats were so dry that we could hardly swallow anything. We tried sucking pieces of ice, but it only made our thirst much more intense. This was our fourth day in the boats, and we had sailed clear of the ice and were at the mercy of the open sea.

All that I remember of that day was trying to keep some warmth in my body. We had our sails set; however, we tried to use the oars thinking that the work would keep us some warmer, but we had little success. As night approached, we could see the ice covered peaks of Elephant and Clarence Islands, which we had hoped to reach before dark. But old Father Neptune was of a different opinion. Probably he thought we needed one more night of punishment to teach us to stay away from his southern domain. We certainly more than received just punishment for our trespassing.

The distance was farther than we had estimated. Darkness came, and to avoid any chance of missing one of the islands, we decided not to proceed any farther. There was nothing to be done but to heave to for the night and such a night as we spent. It grew colder and heavy squalls from the islands lashed the sea with hurricane force.

The boat[35] that I was in was the smallest one. It contained eight men, sleeping bags, grub and the infernal blubber stove, which was always in the way. The larger of the other two boats took us in tow, and that is one reason why I am writing this book. If they had not taken us in tow yours truly and my seven boatmates would be exploring the next world. We were kept very busy all night bailing water. That is the three or four of us who were able.[36] We were constantly shipping water.

It was on that night that I learned what one party of men did when they were certain that death was coming to them. We had shipped considerable water and were slow in bailing it out, when a big white comber broke over us and filled the boat gunnel full. I never felt so sure of anything in my life as I did of death that night. I was certain that my time had come, and speaking for my mates and myself, I will say that there was not an outward sign of fear. I remember remarking

---

[35] *Stancomb Wills*
[36] Bakewell, How, and McIlroy bailed, Crean was at the tiller.

to Crean (the officer at the helm), "Here goes our payday," as a wave lifted us up and it must have been a jerk from the boat towing us that saved us. A lot of the water rolled out and we lost no time, nor did anyone need any urging to bail out the remainder of the water. Although we suffered tortures that one would not think man capable of enduring, we somehow kept afloat until daylight. One horrible nightmare was over.

With the daylight the sea and the wind calmed. Elephant Island was but a short distance and it was a joyful sight to gladden our eyes. Its ice-covered peaks looked like the Garden of Eden to us. As we came closer to the island, good fortune favored us once more. There was very little surf. Sir Ernest got into our boat and we preceded the others to find a place to land. We made a landing on a point, which had a stony beach some forty or fifty feet wide and a sheer cliff rising up from it. The water was very shallow and rocky. We unloaded what stores we carried and five of the men. Blackborrow could not stand[37] and some of the others were in nearly the same condition. Sir Ernest, Crean, How, and I went back and got some of the stores and men from the other boats, making it possible for them to land with safety.

Finally we were all ashore and a more pitiful or forlorn group of men would be hard to imagine.

---

[37] When Blackborow could not stand on his own, Bakewell and How carried him up onto the beach.

Chapter 8
Elephant Island

We had been five days in the open boats, with next to no sleep, nothing to drink, and no warm food for over three days, with the temperature around zero most of the time. The sick were made as comfortable as possible on the beach, and by the time the last boat was beached, the cook had the blubber stove going and got drink made from powdered milk ready for us. "Oh! How good it tasted."

We had noticed a number of seals on the beach when we first landed, and they were soon killed and made ready for the second course of our feast, the blubber being used for fuel. After our drink of hot milk, we started on the seal steaks, and this course lasted until late into the night. After the cook had satisfied our first pangs of hunger, he quit and others took it upon themselves to fry the steaks and melt ice for water. There was always a crowd around the stove eating and drinking, besides trying to dry their clothing.

The day was one of the finest I had seen in the south. The sun shone bright all day, and we managed to dry our sleeping bags and clothing some, but it would have taken many days to get them thoroughly dry. We also mended our gear and did whatever we could for our future comfort. The two doctors were kept busy dressing the fingers of those who had had them frozen. Blackborrow was in the worst condition as his toes were frozen back to his feet. The others had only the ends of their fingers nipped.

There are not words enough with which to describe the contented feeling that I had, and I am sure the others felt the same. If one will stop and think, that was the first time in seven months that we had been where we could feel secure. The rocks, although they were barren, gave us a feeling of security that I know no one can appreciate unless they have floated around on sea ice and in open boats as long as we had.

Somehow, I got one night of rest. I did not sleep much, just lay in my damp sleeping bag and relaxed. It was hard for me to realize that I was on good old solid earth once more. I got up several times during the night and joined the others, who, like me, were just too happy to sleep. We would gather around the fire, eat and drink a little, have a smoke, and talk over some of the past adventures. Later we crawled into our sleeping bags and dozed for a while. The second day on the island was a bright sunny day like the preceding one. There was not much room on the narrow beach for us to build any permanent shelter. There was too much danger of the sea coming up to the cliffs during a blow from the east or south, so Sir Ernest sent a party in one of the boats to see if a better place could be found. They were gone all day and did not return until dark. They found a place seven or eight miles up the coast. The next morning we broke camp and were soon off up the coast to our new campgrounds. I know for myself, I was not in favor or anxious to do any more boating, and many of the others were of the same notion.

The weather had made a change for the worst. We had to buck a headwind and current all the way, and those men who had frost bitten fingers suffered agonies. We made the new camp in good time. It was a sandy spit with a high rocky hill at one end. Not very inviting, but still it was better than our first landing place. A large glacier was just west of us, and the coast consisted of high cliffs as far as we could see. We landed everything safely although there was some surf running. We got our partly dried clothing wet again. There was half sleet and rain falling. We were all very tired, wet, and miserable. We turned our boats upside down for a shelter. We then crawled into our wet sleeping bags, shivered, and slept until morning. The day greeted us with a half rain and sleet. It was the worst kind of weather to be out in, if you have no warm shelter to go to.

Our leader [Shackleton] decided to take the largest boat[38] and try to make South Georgia, and then bring relief to us. The carpenter[39], two other men[40] and I[41] were put to work to make the boat ready for its dangerous trip. With parts from the other two boats and some of the canvas from the tents, we managed to deck it over. It was a very cold job, as we had to work barehanded most of the time. It took a couple of days and a very shipshape job we did considering the material we had to work with.[42]

Sir Ernest, Captain Worsley, Crean, the carpenter [McNish] and two sailors[43] started out on one of the most dangerous trips, I think, that six men ever undertook. It was over eight hundred miles to South Georgia and over the wildest body of water on the face of the earth. They had only a cockleshell of a boat to make the trip in.[44] They started with their sails set and with a westerly breeze, and it was not long until they disappeared over the horizon. We that were left stood in a group and gazed out to sea as long as they were in sight. Then the questions, "Will they make it? and if not, how long will we be able to exist?" I know that is what went through my mind and I am safe in saying that the same thought was with the rest of the men.

We could not afford to lose any time, so Wild (who was left in command) started us right away to build a stone wall about three feet high. It took days to gather the stones. The two boats

---

[38]*James Caird,* 22'6" in length, with a 6 foot beam.

[39]McNish

[40] Marston and McLeod

[41]Bakewell and Greenstreet also sewed bags for ballast. How and some of the other men helped thaw, stretch, and sew pieces of canvas together. This canvas was used to cover the top of the *James Caird.* Several of the men were too ill to help

[42]The results of their effort have been preserved and can be seen on the *James Caird* at Dulwich College.

[43]Shackleton, Worsley, Crean, McNish, McCarthy, and Vincent made up the party of six that left for South Georgia.

[44]While loading the *James Caird* from the *Stancomb-Wills,* McNish and Vincent got soaked. Bakewell and How exchanged clothes with them. It took weeks for those wet clothes to dry thoroughly.

were set on top of the wall, bottom side up, and with the help of the sails, sealskins, rope, and oars we made a fairly weatherproof shelter. The blubber stove was rigged up inside. A stovepipe was made from the tin of one of our food boxes.[45]

Painting commissioned by Elizabeth Bakewell Rajala from Walter E. How, a close friend of William Lincoln Bakewell.

The James Caird rigged up to sail to South Georgia some 800 miles by sea from Elephant Island. Six men aboard and 16 days of sailing the roughest sea in world to reach South Georgia.

We gathered all the penguins and seals that we could get for our food and fuel. We also killed two or three sea elephants. Food was now our big problem. There were twenty-two of us, and every one with a gluttonous appetite. From the large pile

---

[45]The camp (shelter) was often referred to as "the Snuggery." The name is appropriate, as the two lifeboats were smaller than the *James Caird*. Twenty-two men lived in this camp for 4^1/2 months. The camp was roughly 20'x10'. Some of the men slept in the "rafters" and the rest on the floor. The camp also served as an operating room when some of the toes on Blackborow's foot needed amputating.

of meat that we had, most people would think that it would have lasted us indefinitely, but it did not. Now there was nothing to do but wait until the relief ship came.

The ice pack closed in on us, and we were ice locked for months. During that time no penguins or seals were killed. They had moved to some other place. Not being able to replenish our meat and fuel supply, we had to economize very closely.

The time had now passed when we were sure that if the boat party had made South Georgia, relief should have reached us. Therefore, we had that anxiety to add to our worries. Shortly after the boat party left, we had some hard blows so we were afraid that they had been lost. As we all had become very much attached to one another, you can imagine how keenly we felt their loss, and our own safety made double the worry. We were faced with a new hardship. Our tobacco supply was finished. We missed our smokes more than any thing else, as most of us were very heartily addicted to the weed. With next to starvation rations and no tobacco, our minds were always on something to eat or smoke, and in all probability, it was for the best. Had we had plenty to eat and to smoke, our minds would have been on our real peril, which would have been very dangerous to the morale of the camp.

The winter was upon us and the wind blew in a gale most of the time. We would get sudden squalls[46] from off of the glacier back of the camp that would fairly sweep a man off his feet. We constantly had to repair damages done to our shelter by those terrific winds. Pieces of ice were breaking from the glacier all the time. The noise annoyed us greatly at first, but we soon became accustomed to the noises and paid little attention to them. One night there was a tremendous crash and roar, which brought us all to attention. A very large piece of the glacier had broken off and dropped into the sea. The wash of it threw large lumps of ice upon the spit so close to our shelter that there was not any joke

---

[46] These squalls were small whirlwinds, and Bakewell called them "williwaws," which was a term used by seamen who traveled the Straits of Magellan.

about it. If a single one of the pieces had hit us, we would have been smashed into bits. It was a case of a miss is as good as a mile. It was another peril to add to our list.

[The following was written by Walter How for his friend William Bakewell about their life on Eleplant Island while waiting for rescue.

My name is Billy Bakewell.
My shack's on Elephant Isle.
The walls without a single brick.
The roof without a tile.
But never the less I must confess
For man and many a mile
Is the most palatial dwelling place
You'll find on Elephant Isle.]

Our supply of meat had gotten so low that the allowance we were getting did not begin to satisfy our hunger. We were always craving food. When the weather permitted, we would walk back and forth on the spit. This spit is what we called the promenade. Usually there were two or three of us together, and we were always talking about the big feeds we should have if we ever got out of this and into civilization.

One day I had a pleasant surprise. Wordie, one of the scientists, had found enough tobacco among his few personal belongings to make a cigarette. I had been helping him clean a piece of sealskin to fix his moccasins, so he gave me the tobacco. He said smoking did not bother him. I accepted it without hesitation. I knew it would have been suicide to try to smoke it while the rest of the bunch was around. I gave How, who was my chum, a peep at it and a sign to follow. We made tracks around a big rock at the end of the spit and were out of sight. Wild was also there as he had been out to the outward edge of the pack. He had been scouting around to see if he could find any seal or penguins or best of all a ship. I rolled the tobacco into a cigarette, using toilet paper for a cigarette paper. The other two never said a word. I lighted it, took a couple of big draws, and then passed it to them. We were like

Painting commissioned by Elizabeth Bakewell Rajala from
Walter E. How, a close friend of William Lincoln Bakewell.

Life on Elephant Island for 22 men for 4^1/2 months

three kids stealing a smoke. It surely tasted good. It had been months since we had had a smoke, and it made us dizzy We smoked until we burned both lips and fingers. It was amusing to think of how we tried to get a smoke. Some of the men, who smoked pipes, boiled them in water with seaweed. Then dried the seaweed and tried to smoke it but did not get any satisfaction. Doing without tobacco was one of our worst hardships.[47]

We had now been over three months on the island. A westerly wind blew the ice clear of the island, and the only ice in sight were numerous bergs. We now expected that the seals and penguins would once more pay us a visit. One day one of the men was plundering around the rocks along the edge of the water and discovered a new source of food for us, in the form of shellfish called limpets. They cling to the rocks and were procurable only at low tide. In taste, they resemble the oyster or clam. The few we were able to gather were a very welcome change from the meat diet.

Another day while we were all in our shelter, we heard the cry of "clark, clark" and upon rushing out we found two penguins the first we had seen for months. Soon they were captured and added to our scant supply of food. Their return put us into better spirits, and it was but a few days until we killed more and a seal. One day the tide was exceptionally low so we gathered a very liberal supply of limpets. With the very ready consent of our leader, Mr. Wild, we decided to have one good feed. Our five-gallon pot that we used to cook in was filled full of limpets, cut up seal livers, tongues, and meat and put to cook. As it cooked it smelled so delicious. We were all anticipating a feed that would be fit for a king.

Our happy thoughts of food were disturbed by a cry from one of the men who was outside of the shelter. "Ship, there's a ship!"[48] There was a mad scramble by all to get out. In the

---

[47]Another story Bakewell related to his family is that he worked for days digging in a snow bank where a shirt of his was buried. Why? Because there was a bit of tobacco in the pocket. What men won't do for a smoke!

[48] August 30, 1916

rush, the small entrance to our shelter was carried away, and yes, there we could see a ship. We gave one big cheer, and it came right from the bottom of our hearts. They had sighted us and were lowering a boat. What ship it was, what country it was from, or who they could be, we did not care but we were asking each other, "Do you suppose they have come for us?" They were too far out for us to make out what flag was flying on the ship's stern or to read her name, but it was not long before our curiosity was satisfied.

As the lifeboat drew nearer, we recognized Sir Ernest and Crean. Then there were some lively cheers given. It was like seeing some one back from the dead. The first words Sir Ernest spoke were, "Are all hands safe?" When we answered, "Yes", we could see an expression of relief come over his face. The boat crew had their pockets full of cigarettes, which they passed to us and a cloud of smoke was soon issuing from our mouths. McLeod rammed two cigarettes, paper and all into his pipe. It made the best smoke he ever had, so he said.

The lifeboat made three trips before we were all aboard the ship. It was called the *Yelcho* and was from Punta Arenas, Chile. Before we fully realized it, we were under way and Elephant Island was dropping fast astern. I was sure there were no regrets from anyone of us. Probably we were not very grateful for the hospitality the island had given us in our time of need. Some went to the trouble to find our cook, who had already become friendly with the ship's cook. They asked Green (our cook) if he realized that he had left our limpet stew on the fire and that it would burn. "Blankety, Blank, Blank, with you and the stew, and the Blankety Island can burn for all I care," he said.

We soon had our stomachs full of civilized food and drink. The crew certainly did everything for our comfort, but one thing we noticed was that they all kept at a distance. It took us some time to realize that we were not carrying an Eau de Cologne odor with us. We had on the same clothing that was issued to us when we left the *Endurance*. They were soaked with grease and blood;

therefore there was an extremely strong odor about us. We were so accustomed to the smell that we did not notice it.

Painting commissioned by Elizabeth Bakewell Rajala from Walter E. How, a close friend of William Lincoln Bakewell.

The men dreamed of this warm place while they were cold and hungry on Elephant Island.

The *Yelcho*[49] was only a lighthouse tender. This ship was rather small to be on such a dangerous voyage. There was not any fresh water to spare for any washing, so we had to go without a bath until we reached Punta Arenas; of course, that wasn't any hardship for us. There were not enough bunks for all of us, so we just lay down wherever we could find room. I spent my first night on the grating above the engine room. I did not sleep much but sure smoked myself silly. There was plenty to eat and drink. We had extremely nice weather so our trip to civilization was enjoyed very much indeed.

Naturally, one of the first questions that we asked was, "How long had the war been over?" The reply was most disappointing and naturally a great surprise to us. When we were told that one of the cruelest wars in the history of the world was still raging, we were thunderstruck and realized that all our different plans would have to be changed.

---

[49] The remains of the bow of the *Yelcho* are on display in Puerto Williams, Chile.

Credit: Picture taken by Ben Garrett of Victory Cruises. Permission to use granted.

The Bow of the *Yelcho*

The bow of the Shackleton Expedition Chilean Navy rescue ship, *Yelcho*, rests in the square in Puerto Williams, Chile, the "Gateway to Antarctica."

Captain and Pilot of the *Yelcho*, Luis Pardo has a street, PILOTO PARDO, named after him in Puerto Williams, the world's most Southern town.

Yelcho finally rescued the crew of the *Endurance* in August during the dead of winter after several aborted attempts by other ships.

After 4 days of navigation of the Drake Sea full of icebergs, the Captain Pardo entered immediately in the bay where the crew of the *Endurance* was marooned on Elephant Island in the Antarctic.

Pardo rescued them in three trips with the lifeboat.

Saving the last man he put the motor of the *Yelcho* in gear just as the tide was changing and the ice started to close the exit of the bay!

The *Yelcho* just managed to get out.

There probably would have been a different story if the captain had waited a few minutes longer.

Pardo later received many honors from the British Government.

The main street in Puerto Williams, running from East to West in front of the bow and town center where the photo is taken is named *Yelcho*.

Photo taken looking South towards Antarctica which is 700 miles away.

When Sir Ernest told us that the *Yelcho* was the fourth ship with which he had attempted to rescue us, we began to realize the efforts that he had made to get us off the island. The other ships were unable to reach us because of the ice, and had the *Yelcho* been a few days earlier, she would have had the same fate. A westerly wind had blown the ice away, and they reached the island without any trouble.

We made a fast run to Punta Arenas. Here I had my first view of the Straits of Magellan, the rocky island of Tierra del Fuego to the south, the barren shores of Patagonia to the north, and the lofty peaks of the Andes in the distant west. All this made magnificent scenery.

As the city of Punta Arenas hove in sight, I received another surprise. I had expected to see a town of shacks, similar to the western United States or Canadian boomtowns. Instead, I found a fine little city of ten thousand, very much the same as one will see in the central western states.

Large ships could not come up to the wharf as the water was too shallow, but the *Yelcho* was of light draught. We steamed up to the wharf, and there, I was one of a party who received the biggest welcome it would be possible for any town to give. The entire population was there to great us, band and all. No town could have given a more demonstrative or freehearted welcome than did the city of Punta Arenas.

We went directly to one of the hotels, where we had our first bath and complete change of clothing since leaving the poor old *Endurance* eleven months before.

What hardships and dangers we had endured in that time, no one could realize unless placed in the same or similar situation. That was past history, and the present and future were of much more interest to us then.

We were to partake of Chili's hospitality and she certainly knew how to treat her guests. We had to wait two weeks to get a ship to Buenos Aires. The entire two weeks were a continuous round of banquets. We would get up from one banquet only to be taken to another. We landed on Sunday, and the following

Sunday the city gave a picnic for the entire population, in our honor. They killed hundreds of sheep and a few cattle for the barbecue. There were also a number of barrels of beer and wine. They danced the Cueco (quacker), the national dance of Chile. It was a most delightful sight. Hundreds of people were dancing at one time. The women in their many bright colored dresses and the men with their gay colored sashes made a beautiful sight indeed, and we all enjoyed the day very much.

Our stay ended with the arrival of the ship from Buenos Aires. I was not very enthusiastic about leaving as I was having a wonderful time, and I know the other men felt much the same. The people of Punta Arenas were sorry to see us leave. I am afraid there were many of the young women whose hearts were sad or broken when the ship (*Austriana*) sailed.

It took us fourteen days to sail to Buenos Aires. We stopped at six or seven ports to discharge and take on passengers and cargo. At every port, we had more entertainment and on the ship, it was one round after another of amusement. When we landed in Buenos Aires, we had been living the life of Riley for a month, which we thought was about enough, but the many friends of the expedition in Buenos Aires thought differently. We were entertained royally by them.

After a week or more of entertainment, I was faced with the hardest problem of all. When I joined the expedition, I asked that I might be paid off at Buenos Aires on our return. Sir Ernest consented to my wish, and now I was at the parting of the way. I had to say good-bye to the finest group of men that had ever been my good fortune to be with. We had some very hard times together and some very good times. I will say this that each and everyone were just as willing to take their share of the bad as of the good. The best of friends must part. The rest of the men were to go to England, where they all had home ties. I was bound for the south again.

Chapter 9
Patagonia

In Buenos Aires, I met an old Scottish rancher who owned two large ranches in Patagonia, inland from Santa Cruz. During one of our conversations, I told him that I had spent four years on a sheep ranch in Montana. He offered me a position as manager of one of his ranches, as he was too old to tend to both of them. His nephew, who had been manager, had gone home to go to war and had been killed. He offered very liberal wages, also first class passage to Santa Cruz, and back to Buenos Aires.

I very readily consented, as I was anxious to have the feeling of a horse under me once more. I had had my fill of the sea for a while and welcomed the change.

We sailed south on the same ship that I had come from Punta Arenas on. Some of my old shipmates were down to see me off.[50] What I had always thought impossible happened. Old McLeod, one of the most hard-boiled sailors

---

[50] In 1964 Bakewell and his daughter Elizabeth attended the fiftieth reunion of the *Endurance* expedition in London. Sir Ernest Shackleton's second son, Lord Edward Shackleton, hosted the reunion. Six survivors attended. They were William L. Bakewell, Charles J. Green, Lionel Greenstreet, Walter E. How, Dr. Alexander H. Macklin, and Dr. James A. McIlroy. This reunion was of great significance to Greenstreet, How and Bakewell as they had corresponded all through the years. During the reunion, Bakewell found out that McLeod was living in Canada. By the time Bakewell was able to travel to Canada to see him, he found that McLeod had died. Bakewell was sadly disappointed. Several of the men had perished during World War I after returning from the expedition.

After the reunion, Bakewell and his daughter traveled to Newport, Wales to visit the Blackborow family. This was a very emotional visit because Perce and my father were lifelong friends. One of Perce's last letters before he became ill was to my father. From Blackborow's family, Bakewell learned he was responsible for keeping Perce alive when they were in the *Stancomb Wills* during the trip to Elephant Island. Bakewell was very modest and had said little about this.

I ever ran across, started to blubber like a baby when I bade him good-bye. Some of the others' eyes were moist; as for me, I did not cry, but I sure would have liked to. We had been through Hell together, sharing our food, tobacco, and clothing when each was worth its weight in gold to us. We were now parting, and it was very hard to say good-bye. They stood on the dock and waved a last farewell as the ship sailed out of the harbor. That was the last that I saw of them.

The voyage down the coast proved to be ten or twelve days of pleasure for me. The only occupation of Richard Walker, the Scottish chief engineer, seemed to be that of seeing that I had a good time. At the different ports where the ship stopped, Walker exerted every effort to amuse me. At Port Madryn he was so sincere in his efforts at giving me a good time that it took four of us to carry him aboard the ship. The next morning when I came to life, I was in Walker's bunk and he was on the floor asleep. It took me some time to awaken him and several drinks to get some life into him. He asked me if I had had a good time. I told him that by the way my head felt I surely must have had. "Well, that is what we live for," he said. "The headache we will attend to immediately." He called his tiger or steward and gave him an order. The steward returned in a few minutes with an assortment of bottles. Walker proceeded at once to mix an antidote for my headache, and it worked like a charm. It was only a few minutes until I never knew I had such a thing as a headache. We were now ready for another day.

There was one other American on board named Fred Johnstone of Kansas City. He took it upon himself to assist my employer and Walker to see that I should not want for anything. At Puerto Deseado, Johnstone and I went hunting. He was very well acquainted along the coast and said that we should be able to kill some martinets. The martinet is a bird resembling the grouse or partridge. He hired a car and we drove about five miles out from Puerto. He had a shotgun and a twenty-two rifle. He told me to take my choice. I chose the rifle. We went up a dry creek, he on one side and I on the other. We did not go far until I spied a covey of birds. By the description Johnstone had given me, I knew them to be the martinets. They seemed quite tame, as I got to within fifty feet of them, and they kept on feeding. It had been four years since I had shot a gun. I had been called a very good shot, so I was rather excited. I was afraid I would not be able to keep up my record. I let go at the bird that was standing giving me the once over. His curiosity cost him his life. I shot him through the head. Three of his mates soon met his fate before the rest decided to move. When they did move they very foolishly took a course directly over my friend, and he reduced their numbers by three, using both barrels of his gun. Therefore, we had seven nice birds, and we were feeling very much elated. The remainder of the covey lighted in some thick brush between the car and us. As the day was getting very warm, and we were well pleased with our bag, we started back to the car. On the way to the car, Johnstone shot one more bird, but I did not get a shot. We had killed four apiece. We drove back to Puerto and went aboard the ship. Campbell and Walker were waiting for us. Walker took charge of the birds, informing us that they would be served for our dinner that evening. Besides that, he said he and Campbell would see to the rest of the dinner. The dinner was done up in grand style. The ship's chef had done his work well. The birds were cooked fit to please the most critical of epicures and eaten with the choicest wines and liquors that the ship carried. It was not until the wee hours of the morning that we disbursed and then only because the steward wanted to get the dining room cleaned for breakfast. We sure had a wild time. Campbell got to feeling so good that he sang us a song in Gaelic, and if it had not been for the rest of us, he would have danced the Highland fling. We were afraid he would fall. He weighed over two hundred

103

pounds and none of us were in any condition to pick him up. After the request of the steward, we retired and it was late in the afternoon before we came on deck again.

Campbell and Walker were ahead of me, and I found them at the bar. They were looking sick and forlorn. They claimed that the cook had spoiled the birds by seasoning them too highly and that was what made them sick. Of course, the wine and other drinks had had nothing to do with it. I told them that I was feeling fine and they said that there wasn't anything that would make a man sick who had lived on seal blubber as long as I had. It was some time before Johnstone appeared. We had had several drinks and were all looking on the bright side of life when he joined us. He had the same story, bum cook, rotten drinks, and that he would be glad when he got back to the States where he would be able to get a square meal and something fit to drink. By the time we got enough of the medicine that cures all ills down him, he voluntarily admitted that there were worse places in the world than sailing down the Patagonia coast, on board the good ship *Austriana*.

We had one more port at which to stop, Puerto San Julian, before reaching Santa Cruz. We did not resist a little party at San Julian. On board the ship, we had a farewell party the last night of the trip. If there had been any more parties, I am afraid that I should not be here to tell the tale. I managed to survive the party and reached Santa Cruz safely.

Campbell, although he had been away from his ranches for months, was not in any hurry to leave Santa Cruz. I was tired of the high life and was anxious to get astride a horse once more. What I could see of the country from the town looked very much like parts of Montana. Campbell, at last, was ready to depart,[51] so we bade Santa Cruz good-bye and started for his nearest ranch, Agua Chico, which was a three-day journey. Campbell had a light two-wheeled cart, much

---

[51] Latter part of October 1916.

the same as the kind used in the States for breaking horses. I bought two horses, one I rode and on the other I packed my belongings. Campbell said that I did not need to buy the horses, but I did not intend to be caught afoot inland, in case I did not get along with my new boss.

South America

URUGUAY

BUENOS
AIRES

ARGENTINA

CHILE

Patagonia

South Atlantic Ocean

Chico River

Campbell's Ranches
Agua Chico
Santa Cruz

FALKLAND
ISLANDS

Tres Cerros
Ranch

Santa Cruz
River

Punta
Arenas

Ushuaia

Tierra
del
Fuego

Cape Horn

Scotia Sea

(Map by Jim Carter—from National Gographic and other sources)
Permission given to Elizabeth Bakewell Rajala to print.

Patagonia Area showing the Campbell Ranches

105

The first few miles out from Santa Cruz, we traveled through hilly country and then we reached the pampas. Excepting a few small gullies, the pampas are as level as a table, with a gradual slope to the Andes Mountains. Our course was about due west from Santa Cruz. We traveled until late in the evening. We made our first stop at a cantina or roadhouse forty miles from Santa Cruz.

I was just about all in. It had been so long since I had done any riding. I was sore all over. Our refreshments during the day had been from a bottle that Campbell had fetched along. After the riotous living for a month and a half, I was very soft. I knew I would be all right after a few days. We stayed two nights and a day at the cantina. Campbell wanted to rest and visit, so did I. The second lap of the journey I did not feel so bad. We stopped one night at a ranch, and I found that one received the same cordial hospitality as is found in the Western States. As I could not speak but very little Spanish, I felt out of place. Every day I was learning a few words, and it was not long before I could make myself understood. The people at the different ranches were very friendly and glad to see Campbell. He introduced me as his new manger. Naturally, I felt more than a little important. Jumping from an able seaman to the manger of a ranch of two hundred thousand acres, and stocked with forty thousand sheep, seemed too good to be true. Sometimes I thought there was a catch in it, but as I had all to gain and nothing to lose, I did not worry.

The fourth day we reached the first ranch, Agua Chico (small water). The buildings were built of adobe and corrugated iron. The house was roomy and comfortable. At this ranch, there were four men and a cook. By their looks, they were not very glad to see their patron. When I was introduced as the new manger, I could see they were doing some hard thinking. Everything showed that they had not done much work while Campbell was absent. With his return and a new manger, they realized that there would be plenty of work in the near future.

Campbell had given me a fair idea of what was to be done. There was the dead wool from the sheep that had died during the winter months to be bailed, and also from the hides of the sheep that had been killed for food.

The first morning, I set the men to cleaning, and by night, the place looked spick-and-span. Campbell said that the men did more work that day than had been done while he was away. The following day I planned to look at the ranch and sheep in order to see what kind of an outfit I was to manage. Sheep are handled very differently in Patagonia than in the United States. In the States they are run in bands of two or three thousand, with a herder, but in Patagonia they are turned loose in paddocks or pastures. On the Agua Chico ranch, the paddocks were six miles wide and nine miles long, running from the Rio Santa Cruz back. The house and other buildings were about two miles from the river.

I had one of the men bring up the horses, which were kept in a smaller paddock near the house. There were about thirty head and a few young horses that had not been ridden much, as I could not see any saddle marks on them and they were not stoved up. All of them were small and very much like the Indian Cayuse of the United States. Campbell claimed there were twelve young horses that had been broken the year before, but I could only find eight. I did not ask any questions but picked out the meanest looking hide full of tricks in the bunch. He was a chunky little roan or *morro* as it is called in Patagonia. As I picked up a heavy throw rope made of rawhide, I heard a chuckle from some of the men who were standing outside the corral fence. I paid no attention to it. I knew that my future prestige was at stake and that my actions in the next few minutes would mean my failure or success as a manger. I dropped a loop over the morro's head very nicely at my first throw, and with the help of the snubbing post in the center of the corral I hauled my horse in. I worked him up close to the post so that he would not be able to strike me with his front feet, in case that was one of his tricks. He never tried that, and when I put my hand on him, he quivered all over but stood perfectly still. I slipped the bridle on without any trouble, then the saddle, pulled the cinch tight, and still he did not move. I did not like that and knew that he was saving his devilment until I mounted. My big worry was the saddle. It was what they called a Falkland Island saddle. It did not have a horn, and the front and back were alike, just a bare tree. It was used with a sheepskin spread over it and held down with a light cinch. The stirrups were the only good things about the saddle. I wished for a heavy stock saddle with a bulge fork, but it was a case of when in Rome do as Rome does. Before mounting the horse, I applied a little wrinkle that I had learned in Montana, hobbling the stirrups. Tying a rope from one stirrup to the other does this. This is a great help when a horse is bucking. I have never liked to ride a strange horse in a corral as some horses will throw their rider, then kick, and trample the rider to death if possible. I led him outside and instantly he came to life, doing everything possible to keep me off. I had not gone to all my trouble for nothing. I will confess that I am not an expert rider, but have a very good knack for mounting. Therefore, I was up and astride the horse with my feet in the stirrups before he knew what was happening. I was hardly seated when he snapped into action. For the next few minutes (hours to me), I rode as I never had before or since. Everything in me was shaken upside down and I even tasted the last piece of blubber that I had eaten on Elephant Island. He would have thrown me had I not hobbled the stirrups. After a while he quieted, hot and tired, but not more so than I. He had had his turn, so I thought turn about is fair play. I had a short rope that I carried for a quirt, but had not used it, so now I began to belabor him with it, and he went off across country in a lope like any good horse. I had conquered and he knew his boss. From that day on we had no trouble, and he turned out to be as fine a little horse as I have ever ridden.

My plans were to look the ranch over and familiarize myself with the lay of the land, so that when I started to gather the sheep I would know where I was. In my tour of inspection, I found that considerable sheep had died during the winter. The wool had not been picked up. There were a number of sheep with their wool dragging the ground. They had been missed at shearing time. They were so wild that I could not get near enough to see if there were many with the scab. I knew that there must be, as the number of sheep that had been missed would mean very good chances for scab. I could see that things in general had been run in a haphazard sort of way. In other words, the boss was not on the job. I made some plans of what to do providing the boss agreed. It was evening when I rode back to the house. Both the horse and I were very tired and hungry.

The only remark passed by the men upon my return was by Campbell. He said, "I don't think that the morro will try any more monkey shines for a while." I replied, "I guess he will be good for a while now." Supper was waiting so I went in and ate my dinner and supper at one sitting. After we finished eating, I told the boss how things were and what I had planned. I told him that the men had been lying around the bunkhouse too much, and that from now on there was going to be some work done, or some of those hombres were going to hit the trail.

The peons were paid only sixty pesos per month, and I told the boss that we could not expect them to do much work for that and that I would like to raise their pay to seventy-five pesos and make them earn it. All he said was that I hired you for manger and that is up to you. He handed me a checkbook, in which he had previously signed each check saying, "There is all the authority I can give you, and when it is gone, let me know." When I realized the confidence he was placing in me, I resolved to do all in my power to show him my appreciation. I rolled into my blankets that night tired and happy. The future looked very bright to me.

I had given the cook orders to have breakfast at six o'clock and to see that the men were up and ready. It seemed but a minute when I was awakened by the unearthly noise of the cook pounding on a frying pan with an iron rod. I wished that I had not been so hasty in giving my orders. I was still tired and sore from the long ride the previous day, but I jumped up as I thought to set an example, but to my surprise, I found Campbell and some of the men in the kitchen drinking *matte*. Yorba matte or Paraguayan tea is commonly used by the native peoples of South America and a habit soon acquired by the Europeans that immigrated. It is very much like green tea.

After breakfast I told the men about their raise in pay and that more work would be demanded, and they would have to work hard if they expected to remain on the payroll. They were pleased about the extra pay and said that they were not to be blamed if things had been neglected as they were willing to do what ever they were told to do. I found them very willing and they always did what I asked very cheerfully. I started them at once to gather all the wool from the dead sheep, and in a few days, they had the ranch cleaned and in good shape. The wool that they gathered was enough to pay their wages for a long time. My boss was very pleased.

As I had things well straightened out on this ranch and knew the run of things, I decided to go to the other ranch and look things over. That ranch was called Tres Cerros and was about one hundred miles west of Agua Chico ranch. I sent one of the men, called Laguna[52] ahead with a cartload of supplies. The boss said that the supplies would be needed as nothing had been sent there for months. I gave Laguna and the cart a two-day start as he would not travel as fast as the rest of us. Campbell and the cook were to stay at the Agua Chico ranch.

---

[52] Bakewell often told a story about Laguna and the ranch cats. The cats always seemed to disappear. While riding out to check the sheep, Bakewell came upon Laguna roasting something over an open fire. It turned out to be one of the cats: Laguna, tired of mutton, found cats to be a delicacy.

The morning of our departure was cold and windy, with sleet and snow squalls. It was a miserable day to travel on horseback. I was determined that there should be no *mañana* business to the outfit while I was in charge. We kept on our way regardless of the weather. It took us nine hours to make our first stop, at a ranch owned by an Englishman named Watson. He was expecting us as Laguna had passed there the day before. From Mr. Watson I learned that Mr. Campbell was one of the pioneer sheep men in Patagonia. He had brought sheep out from the Falkland Islands some forty years before. At that time there was a market only for the wool. The market for tallow was very unreliable. Sometime later, freezer plants had been established in several of the ports, thus creating a market for the meat. Campbell was, therefore, so used to the old methods that he was slow in taking up the new. As Mr. Watson said, "Too old to change his ways, but you will find him a fine man to work for, and if you work things right, you will be able to convince him of the newer and better way of doing things." Mr. Watson also said that he had plenty of money; therefore, I had nothing to worry about. I was very glad to get this information and felt that I should be better able to manage things.

The next day's journey was a long one, as we wanted to reach a Boliche, called Fortaleza. I will try to give you a description of a Boliche. Fortaleza is situated about halfway between the Atlantic coast and the Andes Mountains. There were only two buildings: a combination hotel and barroom, and a general store. The other building was a bunkhouse. A cable ferry crossed the Santa Cruz River at Fortaleza. The north and south road crossed the east and west road at Fortaleza; therefore, the Boliche is practically in the center of the country. This was the favorite gathering place of the men from all the *estancias* or ranches of that part of the country.

In Fortaleza, I met many men who had no other contact with civilization for years, if one can call it civilization. I also met men from all parts of the world, and many of them had good reasons for not seeking any other contact with their fellow men.

One thing, the people were not troubled with anything that represented law, yet the country was not as lawless as you would think. I found the gathering in Fortaleza very orderly, considering the heavy drinking, guns, and no law but that which they made themselves. I noticed that the men were very civil to each other and seemingly too pleased at seeing each other to quarrel. The only fight or near fight that I saw, was between an Irishman and a native Argentino. The Irishman wanted to fight but the Argentino did not. The Irishman was so very abusive and insulting that the Argentino finally said, "If you want to fight so bad come on, but it will have to be Argentino style." The Irishman replied, "All right, I will fight you any style you want and will lick you at it." The Argentino drew from his sash a knife with an eighteen-inch blade. The Irishman became instantly sober and very pale. He made the excuse that he did not carry a knife. The Argentino offered him his knife saying, "I will lend you mine, and I will borrow one from one of the señors here." The Irishman had given up all idea of fighting and was doing all in his power to restore peace. He was not ready to die, and he realized it would be death if he fought the Argentino. The Argentino was a good sport and laughed it off, but refused to shake hands, saying, "I only shake hands with gentlemen." The Irishman was not long in leaving, and I learned later that he left that part of the country for good. I think that the reason for so little fighting in that part of the world was the love and enjoyment of life. A fight was certain death to one or the other of the fighters.

We did not leave until late in the afternoon of the second day. I knew the men had not had a holiday for a long time and I wanted Laguna to reach the ranch before we did. Also there were a number of men at the Fort, and I took this opportunity to get acquainted.

I was glad that we did not leave sooner, as we had the pleasure of seeing one of the oddest characters that I have ever seen. He was an Englishman and a thoroughbred Cockney. He could speak the Spanish fluently, barring his Cockney accent. He kept the house in an uproar with his crazy antics. I had never before or since run into anyone so amusing.

When, at last, we did start on our way, one of the men complained of his side hurting. He had laughed so much, and the men kept one another amused by imitating the Cockney's antics. When we reached the ranch, we found that Laguna had arrived only a few hours before. He was busy transferring the supplies from the cart to horses and thence to the house. The road was up on the pampas, and the house had been built in the lowland along the river. The bluff up to the pampas was so steep that it was all a horse could do to climb it. A road had not been made to the house. It took the best part of a day to get the supplies to the house. In looking around, I found that a road could be built by winding around a horseshoe bend, in the center of which was the house. It would take a lot of work but it would be worth it and besides keep the men busy. Nevertheless, the road would have to wait until the more important work was finished.

The men of that ranch were glad to meet their *nuevo capataz*. There were six men and a cook at the ranch, and I had four with me, so I had ten men to keep busy. The men that came with me were already acquainted with the men of the ranch. They greeted each other in a very hearty manner as only the Latin races know how to do. Bottles were passed, and it was not long until all were very happy, and the ranch hands were told about the Cockney, which amused them very much.

I told the ranch hands of the raise in pay. Needless to say, they were well pleased, and I found them a fine lot of men to work with; all they needed was a leader. I started them to gathering all the wool that they could find lying around. Wool was much higher in price at that time, and in two weeks they had gathered enough to pay their salaries for a year. I had told them they would have to show Mr. Campbell that they could earn their raise, so the ranch was soon cleaned up, a thing that had not been done for years, if ever.

It was close to lambing time and as the lambing would start at the Agua Chico ranch first, I left one man in charge of Tres Cerros, and took the rest and started for Agua Chico. We had a great time on the road. The men were like a bunch of schoolboys on a picnic. For the next three months, it would all be hard work. Daylight until dark, in all kinds of weather, but it did not dull the spirits of the men.

We stopped at Fortaleza the first night. The men had all drawn some money, but did not do as I expected, get gloriously drunk. Of course they had their drinks but were very orderly. What would surprise one most, were some of the things they bought. As I have mentioned before, a Patagonia Estancia furnishes no luxuries in the line of food. The men bought canned pears, peaches, and anything else that the Boliche had in stock in the line of sweets. Those sweets cost the men about four times what they were worth. The men would take a can of fruit and stir in a can of milk, eat it all, and thoroughly enjoy their feed. This mixture and all that they had to drink of rum and whisky, I thought would surely kill them; nevertheless, to my surprise, they were all ready for the saddle the next morning. They had each bought enough sweets and drinks to fill their saddlebags, to be eaten and drunk on the road.

I have not yet mentioned the large herds of guanacos, the wild llamas of the Andes, also the rhea, similar to an American ostrich, which live on the plains or pampas. The guanacos especially are very good to eat. The natives are very fond of them, and the men with me were counting on capturing some on the way, as there was a great number of young guanacos on the pampas.

The way that the men hunt in Patagonia was new to me. I had always hunted with a rifle, but in Patagonia I rarely saw a rifle. The favorite weapon is the bola and some of the men were real experts with it. They could single out an animal, and if in throwing distance, very rarely missed their mark. The bola is made of three bags filled with shot and with a piece of rawhide three feet long fastened to each bag; the free ends of the rawhide are fastened in a knot, which the thrower holds in his hand. He swings the bola over his head and lets it go in the direction of the animal he wished to catch. It is very easy, so they told me, but the only success I ever had was catching my horse and throwing both of us, consequently making me loose all desire to become a bolador. The men caught several of the young guanacos, and they certainly are fine eating. The older ones are strong and very tough and are eaten only in an emergency.

We reached the Agua Chico in good time, as our hunting had not delayed us. We kept three of the guanacos to eat at the ranch, and Mr. Campbell was very much pleased, as he liked them as well as the natives did.

When I told Mr. Campbell the amount of wool we had gathered at the Tres Cerros, he was surprised. He told me that I had gotten more work out of the men than he had ever been able to. I told him my plans for a road from the pampas to the house on the ranch Tres Cerros. He said, "When you get it finished so I won't have to walk up and down the hill I will pay you a visit and not before."

Chapter 10
Reunited with "Red"

Shearing time came soon after the marking of the lambs. In Patagonia, the shearers come to the ranches as each ranch has its own shearing sheds. In Montana, we had to drive the sheep miles to the shearing sheds. The shearers in Patagonia were a cosmopolitan lot, coming from Bolivia, Peru, Uruguay, Falklands, Chili, Argentina, and Scotland. These men drift from one part of the country to another, from the Rio Negro in the north to the Straits of Magellan in the south. Some even go to the Tierra Del Fuego Islands. They are very happy and carefree, at home any place they stop. They earn big wages and accumulate quite a large sum of money in a short time, only to spend it in the many Boliches (old country stores).

After shearing came the dipping of the sheep. That is very hard work, and I spent from fourteen to sixteen hours each day in the saddle, to see that the men did not miss any of the sheep either at the shearing or dipping. When the dipping was finished, the men and horses were pretty well worn out, as my policy was, "Every job thoroughly done." As I knew that both ranches were well cleaned, I told the men that we would take a month's rest. The horses were turned into a large paddock to graze. At the end of the month, we would dip again. I had planned to dip five times that season in order to clean out the scab, instead of three times as had been the custom before.. It would be a lot of hard work and expense but the results would be worth it. Thus, I decided to take a few days rest and forget the sheep.

The snow-covered peaks of the Andes were visible from the Tres Cerros ranch and naturally I wanted to get a closer view of them and if possible climb some of the peaks. Some of the men said that there was a pass in the mountains about sixty miles from the ranch, but very difficult to cross. If one was successful in crossing, it was only a short distance to the settlement of Porta Bordos. My plans were to try to cross the pass and spend a few days in the settlement. I had brought my horses from the Agua Chico ranch, and they were in very fine condition. Early one morning I started out. I packed my camp outfit and provisions on one horse and rode the other. The weather was ideal, the wind was not blowing as strong as usual, and the sky was a beautiful clear bright blue. A few hours' ride and I was clear of the west boundary of the ranch and was traveling over new country. The level pampas were giving way to a slightly rolling country, cut up with small gullies and ravines. The grass was much better than on the pampas. The vast herds of guanaco had disappeared but there were great numbers of martinet. I rode through flocks of them and they did not pay any more attention to me than the barnyard fowls would. They are very tame and during the day I killed two with my six-shooter. At night, I camped on the bank of the Rio Santa Cruz, cooked the martinet, and enjoyed my supper very much. While roaming along the river I noticed every little while fish jumping. I could not make out what kind they were, but by their actions I knew that they were a species of the trout or salmon. Different men whom I had asked about the fish in the river all gave the same answer. "Yes, there are lots of fish, but they can be caught only in a net." They said that they had tried baits of all kinds but no success with a hook and line. As I did not have a hook or line with me I had to give up, but I saved some of the feathers from the martinet to be used in the near future. I am very fond of fish, and I was determined to try to catch some of the fine ones that I had seen in the river. Darkness came on very quickly, so I spread my blankets and rolled in. My thoughts were on the many fine fish that I had caught, the different ways I had caught them, and plans for catching some more. Before I could perfect my plans, I fell into a dreamless sleep that lasted until morning. Oh! what a morning.

The sun was reflecting a million sparkling colors on the snow-capped peaks of the Andes. A more perfect panorama I do not believe could exist. For miles and miles to the north and south there was nothing to obscure my view. I had never seen anything like it before or since, nor do I ever expect to. Light feathery clouds floating over the sun would shroud the picture much the same as a curtain in the theater makes a change from one scene to another; only to show off the grandeur more perfectly each time. I wish that I had the vocabulary sufficient to express the beauty, grandeur, and magnificence of the scene. I doubt if any artist could do its majestic beauty full justice or any author describe it adequately.

That day is one that I shall remember as long as I live, for in it I received the biggest surprise that I have ever had. Mother Nature had exhibited her beauty before me, and as I lay very comfortably in my blankets, I became so engrossed in looking at the wild majestic beauty before me, that I did not hear, as my back was to them, or see the group of riders approaching.

The first I knew of their presence was the greeting. "Ola amigo!" This brought me out of my trance, and upon looking around, I saw seven horsemen but a few rods from me. Seven more desperate characters I had never met. Each had long mustaches and about a month's growth of beard. One was very much different in appearance, as he had a very thick red beard, while the others had straggly black beards. I recognized him as an old acquaintance whom I had met in Gerlach, Nevada. As I stood up to meet them, I greeted him with, "Hello Gerlach Red." He just about fell off his horse and greeted me with, "Well I be damned, if it ain't Montana. How in the hell did you get down in this part of the world?" I answered him by asking the same question. For the next few minutes, we tried to tell how it happened, both talking at the same time.

We were sure two excited hombres. It was certainly good to meet someone that I had known in God's country. Red was like a kid on Christmas morning, and I was beginning to believe in miracles. Red was the last person in the world that I ever expected to see again and least of all in that part of the world. After our excitement died down, Red told the rest who I was and how I had befriended him back in the States. They were apparently glad to meet me. One of them galloped over the hill and in a short time returned with sixteen extra horses and one other man. Most of the horses were carrying packs. The men soon unloaded, and when finished, it looked like a general store; I soon found out that it was the best part of the stock from a Boliche, which they had robbed. The Boliche was a two-day ride south of us. This was the first time that they had stopped as they had been pursued, but they had shaken off their pursuers over in the edge of the mountains by cutting back towards the more level country. They were now safe, and Red said, "Right here is where we camp for a few days and celebrate," and we certainly did. They had every delicacy that the country offered in their loot, and they all wanted to heap the best of everything upon me. This was my first experience as a guest in an outlaw's camp, and I was the cynosure of the camp. For three days all we did was eat, drink, and talk. I told them all about my rambles in the Antarctic and the ships that I had been on, as well as my present position as manager of a sheep outfit. Red told me how he had *borrowed* a Basque sheepherder's horse and rode out of Gerlach the night after I left there. He also told me how he *traded* for different horses during the night until he had reached the Mexican border. On his trip through Mexico he met a Chilano who told him of the fine pickings they could have down in South America. They went to the Port of Manzanillo, and from there to a port in Peru where they went to work relieving people of their belongings.

They worked their way south through Chile. The Chilano was still with him. The rest of the gang were Peruvians, Bolivians, and two other Chileans.

I shall not tell here all of Red's story, perhaps some other time. Don't judge him too severely as he was just a victim of circumstances. I know his start and something of his finish. That was their second raid through that part of the country. The first time, they had robbed a bank in Rio Gallegos. On the second raid they were keeping close to the mountains, as they could elude their pursuers easier, and if they were compelled to fight, they could find better protection. Of course, they did not get as rich a loot from the Boliches as they would have in the seaport towns, but they were playing safety first. Red said that the Boliches were only legalized robbers, so he did not have any regrets for relieving them of their stocks. He did not bother any of the working men or the Estancias, unless it was to get fresh horses, and then he always left horses to replace those that he took. He always avoided any killing unless it was absolutely necessary for their safety. For bandits they were not as bad as they might have been. Red told me if I wanted to, he would be glad to have me join them. He said at the same time that I would be a fool to do so, as sooner or later he would get what was coming to him. I agreed with him that I was better off as I was, and that I had always gotten along fine by staying on the right side of the law, yet got plenty of excitement out of life. As for money, I told him that I had enough to satisfy my few desires. On the third day after our meeting, I bade them good-bye and wished them all good luck. I went directly back to the Tres Cerros ranch as I did not care to meet up with any posse that might be looking for Red and his gang. I did not speak Spanish well enough to explain to strangers my presence in the hills at that time.

I reached the ranch early in the evening as I did not loiter on the way. The men were back from their holiday and did not seem any the worse for wear. I did not tell them anything about my experiences, except those of the martinet and the fish. They just laughed. I said to myself, "He who laughs last, laughs the hardest, and we will see who laughs tomorrow night." As the next day was Saturday, I told the men that we would not do any work until Monday, and then we would start the road. Before going to sleep, I completed my plans for catching the fish. The next morning, while looking for material to make my fishing tackle, they looked at one another, and I know they thought I was loco. From the bright nickel plated cover of the clock I cut out a piece that resembled a fish about three inches long. From parts of the works I made a very passable swivel. I then proceeded to wreck the only stub of a broom that we had on the ranch, using some of the wire. My next problem was a hook. There was not a fishhook on the place. The best material I could find were some nails from a box. With a lot of labor and a dull file I managed to make the nails into the shape of fishhooks. I had everything together to make a spinning minnow and a fly hook from the martinet feathers. If the fish would not take the spinning minnow, I would try the fly hook. For a line I used a heavy linen thread, three strands twisted together and waxed with a piece of mutton tallow. I made my fish pole by splicing pieces of thorn bush together. My outfit being completed, I started for the river, with all hands, including the cook, following me. Their curiosity had gotten the better of them, or probably, as they thought, I was loco, and they had better go along to see that I did not harm myself.

The sun was about an hour high when we reached the river. When I made my first cast, the men could not understand what I was trying to do. I was in luck as it took only a few casts to land a nice fish, some ten inches long. I called it a salmon trout; whether I was right I do not know. For the next hour all I did was haul in fish to the delight and astonishment of the men. It was their first experience in that style of fishing. The fish would take either the spinning minnow or the fly hook.

That night for the first time in many months we had our fill of fish. I had my laugh as I told them that was the way we caught fish in the States. Their only comment was, "Los Americanos del Norte son muy progresivo," or in other words what we go after we get. They were not long in fixing up a fishing outfit, and from then on we had many fine feeds of fish, giving us a great relief from our mutton diet.

Monday we went to work on the road. The men, by that time, were very enthusiastic about it. By the end of the week we had made a trail wide enough for a horse to use. The horses soon learned that it was easier to come down the trail than to slide down the hill on their haunches when they came from the pampas for water. It was quite interesting to watch the long string of horses winding their way down the hillside. The second week we made the trail wider but not yet wide enough for a cart. We had to stop as it was time to dip the sheep again. When we finished dipping the sheep at Tres Cerros, we went down to the Agua Chico and dipped there. Mr. Campbell was more interested in the road and the fish that we had caught than the work among the sheep.

The summer [1917] was spent in going back and forth from one ranch to the other. In between dipping times, we finished the road. When Laguna brought the first cart load of supplies down the road to the house, there was much rejoicing. Mr. Campbell paid one visit to the Tres Cerros ranch and spent quite a little time in inspecting our work. He made many unnecessary trips up and down the road. I am sure that he enjoyed it, and just as sure that the horses did not enjoy pulling the cart back and forth. He stayed only a few days, as it was much colder at the Tres Cerros and the house was not so good as the one at the Agua Chico. I was left all to myself, and all the talking I did had to be in my very poor Spanish. So you may be sure that when I was at the Agua Chico ranch it was a pleasure to have someone to whom I could talk to in my own language.

The summer was over and there was little work to be done-some repairs to the fences and an occasional look at the sheep. If there was a severe storm, we had to drive the sheep from the pampas to the lower and rougher land along the river. The winter was very mild, so we did not have any trouble.

There is a small fox in Patagonia called the Zorra la Pampa. It is similar to the kit or prairie fox and is the easiest animal to trap that I have ever seen. All the foxes that I have had anything to do with were extremely hard to trap, and only an expert trapper with a well-concealed trap could have any success. The Zorra la Pampa would walk into a box trap, one similar to what the North American farm boy uses to catch rabbits; the box trap was what the natives used. Each of the men had three or four box traps, and they were catching quite a number of the foxes before I took any interest in it. I decided that if the foxes were so foolish as to walk into a box trap that I would try a simpler method. I did not say anything to the men, but made about thirty snares using some light fence wire rigged to a spring pole. I had a snare set at every thorn bush that was handy and large enough. These snares worked like a charm. The next day after I set them, I had five foxes. I rather dislike to call them foxes as they are anything but foxy. When I returned to the house with my catch, the men were aghast with wonder, and all wanted to know how I had caught them. When I told them how, and taking a piece of wire, I showed them how easy it was. They all started to talk at once, and Spanish was flying so fast that I could understand only a little of what they were saying. The bulk of the conversation was aimed at poor old Laguna. I thought they were going to eat him. It took sometime for me to figure out why they were so riled. The whole story is that they could see why the North

Americans and English were so much wiser than the Spanish. As Laguna was the oldest, they were putting the blame on him for not knowing and being able to teach them. Laguna denied any connection with the Spanish race and said, "Yo es absolutamente Indian puro." When the men remarked that it was no wonder then that he did not know anything, Laguna was ready to fight, and it took a lot of talking on my part to straighten things out. I did not want bad blood between them. I told them that I had learned to trap from an old experienced trapper and that there were very few Americans that would know how to catch a fox in a box trap. Furthermore, I doubted that the English would know what to do with a fox if they did catch one. I told them of a plan that I had. This was to pool all the skins and when sold, divide the money between them. They would not agree unless I would take my share. Laguna came to the rescue with a very good plan. He suggested that we pool the skins and every other Saturday send one man to Fortaleza, where they were paying three pesos apiece for the skins. The money would be spent for canned fruits and other delicacies, including a few bottles of liquor; therefore all would have a fine time and have no further reason for fighting.

They asked me if I had any more schemes, and if so to come clean, as they did not want to be taken by surprise again. Also, they realized now how much they had to learn. I showed them how to make deadfalls and some other traps. This pleased them very much. Their only means of killing game were the bolas, dogs, or guns, if they were lucky enough to have a gun. A rifle cost around one hundred pesos, or more than a month's pay. It was only since the war had started that the peons on the Estancias could get work for more than six months in the year. At many ranches they were paid only during the lambing, shearing, and dipping times; otherwise the rest of the year they lay around, glad to get enough to eat. After the war began, they were paid the year around; although the pay was small, it was better than what they received before the war. Like everywhere, the price of all commodities had gone up. The peons are a happy, carefree people, very easily offended, but splendid workers when handled properly.

It was eleven months since I had started to work for Mr. Campbell. I liked the work and the rough and ready life of the ranch suited me to perfection. As in all places, the notion to ramble came. I made a hurried trip from Tres Cerros to Agua Chico and found the only mail awaiting me that I received while in Patagonia. There was a letter for me from the British Consul at Rio Gallegos, informing me that he had received a communication from Misters Huston and Cuff Solicitors, Lincoln Inn, London, to pay me for my services on the *Endurance*. I had not received my pay from Sir Ernest when I left him in Buenos Aires. I did not expect my pay until the war was over. The letter was a great surprise to me; however, it was not the letter that put me in the notion of leaving.

Mr. Campbell had received some English papers, and from them I learned for the first time that the United States had declared war on Germany. I decided to go at once, and when I told Mr. Campbell, he said it was no more than he expected me to do, and that he would go if he were younger. I would have entered the British service upon leaving the expedition, only everyone said that the war would be over soon. I stayed out as I did not care to spend a lot of time in a training camp only to find the war ended when I was ready to see some action. Since the United States had entered, I felt that the war would last longer than was realized, so I now determined to get into it.

Mr. Campbell was very sorry to see me leave [late 1917], but he was thankful that he had been able to have me as long as he did. We settled up everything, and I did not have to remind him of the return fare to Buenos Aires. I have heard a lot about Scots being so very close, but my experience with them has been very much the opposite.

Once more, I had the painful task of bidding friends goodbye, and as I did, I knew I was making a foolish mistake. I was earning my living in a neutral country, and as I did not start the war, it would be damn little thanks I would get for helping to finish it. I knew that I should not be able to get as good a situation as I was leaving, but go I must.

Pay Check Authorization from Ernest Shackleton

Of all the places that I had been, Montana and Patagonia suited me best. I was happy and contented. In either place, I could follow the life I liked best and probably a life that I am best suited for. I have never had any desire for the more civilized places, and now I was going back to civilization to play some part in their game of devastation, carnage, and very likely poverty. I was leaving happiness and prosperity behind, but such is life.

My journey back to the coast was not as pleasant as the journey out a year ago. I reached Santa Cruz on the third day, received my pay from the expedition that had been forwarded from Rio Gallegos. I was now all set to go, but the coastwise ship to Buenos Aires had departed the day before I arrived, and there would not be another for two weeks. I did not like to wait but there was nothing else to do. When the ship came I was very glad to bid the city of tin shacks goodbye, as the two weeks had made a very noticeable inroad into my capital.

The ship that I had missed was the one that I had made two trips on, up and down the coast. I was sorry to have missed it, as I had friends aboard her. The ship I took was very much pro German. It belonged to the Hamburg, South American Line, however, sailing under the Argentine flag. I booked passage for Buenos Aires and on the way led a very quiet and conservative life. The only place that I spent much time ashore was at Puerto Madryn, where I had some friends. Puerto Madryn was settled by a colony of Welshmen, who had left their native land when the cruel English made it compulsory for them to teach English in their schools. All of them whom I met spoke English and those who were able had sent their children to England to be educated. This I thought a very odd thing to do considering the circumstances under which they had left their native land. In a previous visit to Puerto Madryn, I had met an American (a sea captain) and his wife. They ran a hotel. As co-patriots, we had a great deal in common to talk about. I also received some very interesting information there about another acquaintance of mine. I met a young Welshman who had a deep fresh scar across his cheek. I thought he had been in the war, but he said, "No", and that he had no desire to go. He told me that he had been working inland in a settlement, where one night while in the commissary store of the settlement, a band of bandits made a raid. The manager was killed and he received the wound that caused the scar. He blamed the manager as he started the shooting. The bandits robbed the store and got safely away. From his description, it was Red from Gerlach, Nevada. Red was still at his old tricks. I must admit that I felt sorry for those who had come in contact with the bullets from his gun, but I was glad that Red was still above the ground. Once more I was not far off Red's trail, although we did not meet that time.

Puerto Madryn was our last stop before reaching Buenos Aires and it was my last visit there. We docked at Buenos Aires early one morning. The city surely looked beautiful with its tree-lined streets, such a difference between it and the treeless pampas of Patagonia. I have had enough experience in the world to know that all that glitters is not gold. All the beautiful tree-lined streets, the lovely plazas, and the magnificent buildings are all right if one had a mint of money so that he might enjoy all the glory those things afford. If he is destitute, it is a different story. Buenos Aires is a city where money soon disappears.

As soon as I found a room, I went to look for a ship and found it much different on account of the war. The first difficulty was a passport or sailor's permit. The American Consul or Vice Consul would not give me a passport without a birth certificate and some other papers that I had never heard of before. I soon learned that the only way to get an American ship out of Buenos Aires was to go to an American

Negro named Brown. He was running a boarding house for sailors down on the Boca. If I paid him twenty-five dollars, I would have no trouble in getting a ship or passport. Well, I had so far in my rambles never had to pay for a job and I was not going to start now. Furthermore, no Negro was going to get twenty-five dollars from me, if I never got a passport. I was one man that they would not get any graft from. As the saying goes, "Where there is a will there is a way," and as my name is Will, I soon found a way through the British Consul. He gave me a seaman's permit and did not ask many questions, all of which I was able to answer without any trouble.

A British ship was all I would be able to get. I wanted to get up to the States, but try as I might I could not. I first tried to get on a Lambert and Holt ship bound for the States, where I intended to leave it and write home for my birth certificate and the other papers that I would need in order to get an American passport.

Chapter 11
Adventures at Sea

I shipped on a Houlder Bros. Ship loaded with frozen meat, bound for some port in Europe. Needless to say, I did not learn the name of the port until we were many days out at sea. The destinations of the ships were kept secret, and the sailors did not get much information about where they were going until they reached the port or were near it.

We finally learned that we were bound for Salonika [Thessaloniki], Greece, by way of the East Coast of Africa with a stop at Cape Town for bunkers. The passage across the South Atlantic was good, as the weather was fine. We reached Cape Town early one morning. As there was no shore leave, we lost no time in coaling the ship, and by night, we were on our way. I would have liked to go ashore and looked around, but that being impossible, all I could see was a jumble of buildings and ships with Table Mountain in the distance. We were not long in rounding the Cape of Good Hope and swiftly steamed up the East Coast through the Mozambique Channel. There we ran into some infernally hot weather. While down in the Antarctic, at times, I thought I should never get thoroughly warm, and while in the Red Sea I was sure I should never cool off. It was somewhat better when we got through the Suez Canal.

At Port Said, we had to wait for a convoy. We managed to get ashore for a few hours, and of course, we saw some ancient women dancing the Can Can. Port Said, from what I saw of it, could stand a very thorough cleansing morally. There, every nation is represented with the immoral people of each nation. We were there only one night, enough for me. The next day found us sailing in a convoy with seven other ships, escorted by two small cruisers. We were once more running in fine weather, but now had the [German] submarines and mines to worry us.

Luck was with us. We did not sight any submarines or hit any mines. Therefore, we had a very pleasant trip up the Aegean Sea. We saw many islands but no signs of the enemy. We reached Salonika without any trouble, only to find once more that we could not go ashore. The captain said there was too much rioting and disorder, and that neither officers nor crew could go ashore. That was very disappointing as I always enjoy looking around a new city or country. I bought some fruit and a few bottles of wine from the stevedores, this being the only chance to spend any money in the port. As soon as our cargo was discharged, we lost no time in getting out to sea, and we were very glad as there isn't any pleasure staying aboard a ship while in harbor. We were soon back through the Suez and down the sweltering Red Sea with a short stop at Aden for coal. An endless chain of near-naked humans loaded the coal. They used small baskets, carrying them on their heads. Men and women were working on an equal basis. It was an odd and interesting sight, watching women carrying little babies in packs on their backs and baskets of coal on their heads. It seemed an odd way to load coal, but surprising how quickly our required amount was loaded. Although the day was extremely hot, I enjoyed the oddity of it very much. No, it was not the near-naked women, as there was not one of them that would cause a white man to leave home or the most disreputable sailor to leave a hungry English ship.

Being out at sea once more, away from that furnace like heat, was a great relief. Our ship was good for sixteen or eighteen knots per hour, and it was only a few days until we crossed the line and were in a cooler and more livable climate.

We were bound for Buenos Aires for another load of meat. I had become reconciled to the fact that my part in winning the war would be on board a ship. But I should like to get to England or France and see how the war was going on. The other sailors aboard who had been over in the danger zone were glad to keep away from it if they could. I was curious and wanted to have a whirl at it. We made a fine run and in due time, were back in good old Buenos Aires, which was beginning to seem like home to me. I was glad to get ashore and have a good meal with a bottle of Vino Chianti. English ships were noted for poor food; the one we were on, however, was a little better than most of them.

I had chosen as my chum a sailor named George. His surname he would not tell me as he said I could not pronounce it. He had carried it twenty years and could not pronounce it properly. He was from Riga, Latvia. He was one of the best natured fellows that I have ever run across, but when once riled, he was very much the opposite. He was over six feet tall and built in proportion, and as for strength, he was a second Sampson. One night we were in a café and one of the waitresses tried to shortchange George by giving him change for a peso bill instead of a five peso bill. George was not going to have it that way. He grabbed her by the arm and told her to come across with the other four pesos. She screamed, and a bouncer came and was fool enough to try to throw George out. The fun started then. George simply picked him up and tossed him over the bar, landing him on the back among the many bottles and glasses. This caused some real excitement. The proprietor was at the door blowing his head off on a police whistle. One waiter was calling the police over the telephone, and the waitress who had caused the trouble was yelling bloody murder. In all, quite a noise was generated. I tried to get George to leave but he would not until he received the balance of his money. He said he did not care if he got ninety-nine years, he was going to get his four pesos. The police came in; one was very heavily decorated in brass buttons and a long sword. There were six other police not so heavily decorated. They all wore Kaiser style spiked helmets. I thought the German Army had invaded Buenos Aires. The proprietor told his trouble in a few words, and the officer ordered his men to arrest George. The officer in charge kept in the background, which I thought showed good judgment. It took all six of the men to take George, and they had a real battle. They finally tripped him with a chair, and while he was down, all six jumped on him. The officer had to keep urging his men on. They wanted to use their swords, but the officer said six men should be able to take one without their swords. I enjoyed the battle and helped by holding George's coat. The police took George and went to the calaboose. I followed as I still had the coat. The officer asked me how it started, and when I told him, he said, "That café is crooked and I do not think George will get much for smashing things; nevertheless I will lock him up for the night and you also for a witness." He put us into what I suppose would be called a patio: wall all around with doors opening into cells. We were not, as I expected to be, locked in a cell. In the patio were two long benches but they were already occupied by some earlier arrivals. George proceeded to dump one over. The occupant protested so loudly that the police came to the barred door to see what was wrong. When they saw George and I stretched out on the bench, using our coats for pillows, they laughed. I heard one of them remark, "Esta hombre uno dablo." We were not disturbed any more, and the rest of the night passed very quickly. I awakened at daylight and began wondering what the outcome of our previous night's rumpus would be. I had plenty of money to pay the cost, but did not like the idea of spending it that way, as there were too many pleasant ways of spending money.

Soon tiring of my thoughts, I awakened George, and he was soon wondering what was awaiting him. Our meditations were interrupted by the officer who had brought us in, with this greeting, "Buenos dias, Jacka Johnston, que querre esta manana?" I told him that we would like to get out. I also asked him how long it would be before we knew our fate. He replied that if my mate was through fighting, we could see the commissioner right away. I told him that George would be all right now, and that I was sure he would not try to annihilate the police force. The officer escorted us into the presence of a very official looking man of middle age, who asked what the charge was. It took the officer about fifteen minutes to tell him. He talked so fast that I could understand but little of what he said, but by the motions that he went through I could see that he was describing the battle at the café. His demonstrations were bringing smiles to the chief and before he finished, the chief was laughing loudly. When the officer finished, the chief asked him what I was arrested for. The officer hesitated a minute, and I answered that I was carrying George's coat. The chief sat for about five minutes just sizing up the two of us; scratching his head he said, "Vamus," and we did. The chief was surely a good sport. The officer escorted us out and accompanied us down the street to the first café, where we had three drinks, each paying for a round. The officer asked us where we intended to spend the day. I told him that we would just be knocking around as we would only get bawled out for being late, if we went aboard the ship at that time of the day. We were going to make a day of it; besides, George wanted to get his money. "That is right" he said, "I had forgotten about that, come on and I will go with you." As it was too early for the other employees to be on duty, we sat down at a table and George called for a drink. The proprietor quickly brought drinks and as he put George's down George grabbed his hand and said, "Give me my four pesos." I knew by the way the proprietor looked that his hand was getting one very hard squeeze. He did not understand George, and I told him that George wanted his money or there would be more trouble. George could not speak any Spanish. The proprietor came through with the money and many apologies, putting the blame on the waitress. To show us that he was all right, he brought a bottle of Vino Mendosa, and we drank it and departed. Our newfound friend, the policeman, insisted that we accompany him to a nice quiet café that he knew and have dinner with him. We agreed, and had one of the best meals that I ever had in Buenos Aires; I ate that day.

After dinner, our friend bade us goodbye as he had to get some sleep before going on duty that night. He told us to be sure and look him up, whenever we were in Buenos Aires, which we promised to do. George and I spent the rest of the afternoon in a movie where I saw my first Charlie Chaplin picture. The evening we spent going from one café to another and at midnight went on board the ship.

The next morning we both expected to get a good bawling out and to be logged one day's pay, but we were in luck. The ship was sailing for Ensenada to finish loading her cargo, as the water was too low for her to load to capacity in Buenos Aires. In the hustle and bustle, our absence was not mentioned.

The run to Ensenada was only a short one of fifteen or twenty miles; therefore, we were soon along side the docks at the Frigrifico, loading the rest of our cargo of frozen meat. We all went ashore that night, but like most small factory towns in the States, Ensenada did not have much to offer in the way of amusement. The next morning we finished loading the ship and were soon on our way with Europe as our destination. As soon as we were out of the Rio Plata, we headed north, so I knew we were bound for England or France. We should soon be in that part of the world that was attracting so much attention.

The days passed very quickly, and it was not long until we were in the danger zone. We were now sailing with all lights out and a double lookout. George and I were doing quartermaster watch, two hours wheel and two hours standing by on the wing of the bridge on the lookout. One night while doing my two hours on the lookout, the mate sent me to tell the firemen, whose quarters were on the after part, to close a deadlight[53] which they had open. It was letting a light shine out. I went and delivered the mate's message and their answer was, "Tell the mate to go to Hell." When I told the mate their reply he just said, "That is too warm a place to suit me."

---

[53] Deadlight—a strong shutter, usually of iron, to protect a cabin window or porthole in stormy weather.

George said to the mate, "If you will let Bill take the wheel, I will go and see that the deadlight is closed." The mate agreed, and it was only a few minutes until we heard a commotion on the after part of the boat deck. Shortly George returned and said, "The deadlight is closed, Sir." He then relieved me at the wheel, and from that time on there wasn't any trouble about the deadlight being closed. The next morning I noticed that several of the firemen looked the worse for wear, and that George had a bruised knuckle on one hand. I suppose closing the deadlight did it.

We were getting near the mouth of the English Channel. A big change had come over all hands. The men were more respectful to the officers, and the officers were more civil to the men. It was not hard to see that all were under a great strain as at any moment a submarine or a mine might mean the finish. The sea was very calm, and we passed a great deal of wreckage, which showed plainly the work of the enemy. We had many false alarms. Once, what we were sure was a floating mine turned out to be a half submerged barrel, and the periscope of a submarine was just an old paint can. But one never knew what minute we might see the real thing.

We reached Brest safely and had to wait for a convoy. We laid out at anchor. I wanted to go ashore as there were many of my countrymen in Brest, and there was a mere chance I might see someone whom I knew. I was disappointed. We were escorted from Brest up the coast, traveling only in the daytime, staying one night at Cherbourg, and another at Le Havre. From Le Havre we went to Boulogne which was our destination. It was a big relief to get into what we thought was a safe port. There we were allowed to go ashore. We had to have passes and for once, I knew a British captain that put himself to a great deal of trouble to accommodate his crew. We had our passes before night and the biggest surprise of all was when the captain told us that those who wanted to draw some money could do so. Very few British ships give money to their crew when in foreign ports. Money did not worry me as I had plenty.

The British Army Base was located at Boulogne. There were soldiers from every part of the British Domain, many of them in their native uniforms, which made a queer sight. Hindus, Kelties, Australians, and also a Chinese labor corps in their queer uniforms. All these looked out of place among the other soldiers in their natty khaki uniforms. Nearly every person on the streets had a uniform of some kind. On a hill south of Boulogne, was the British Camp, where these many different soldiers were quartered. It was referred to as John Bull's Menagerie.

The docks were pilled high with munitions of war. There were signs of activity in every direction. The Old World was moving quickly for once. There was a spirit of adventure everywhere. I for one enjoyed the activity. It was a radical change for me. So different from anything that I had ever seen. Any direction one would look there were signs of life. It was very fine to look at, until one stopped to think and then realize the purpose of it all; it meant the taking of lives, so there was nothing good about the whole thing.

During our first night ashore, we had a funny experience. About nine o'clock we heard bugles blowing and the soldiers all disappeared in double quick order. We thought that it was their call to return to camp, but we were mistaken, as we soon discovered. A red cap ordered us aboard our ship, telling us that there would be an air raid before long, and that we had better beat it while the going was good.

Our ship was only a short way from where we were and in less time than it takes to tell it, we were aboard and none too soon: when bang, whang, sip, boom, and the air raid was on. That was my first experience of war, and I thought every explosion was a bomb from the raiding airplanes, but it was not. The anti-aircraft guns were doing most of the shooting. The Germans had dropped only a few bombs and were off. They did very little damage and none of any military value. I was not long in learning that the greatest danger in the air raids was from the fragments of the shells from the anti-aircraft guns, as they dropped all over. The first thing to do was to get under cover when the warning was given. The next morning after the first air raid we picked up as much as half a deck bucket full of the broken shells. After our first experience, we lost no time in getting aboard ship whenever the bugles gave the warning of an air raid. During our stay in Boulogne we were in five raids.

We were in Boulogne fourteen days. The British could handle only so much meat each day. We were glad when our cargo was finally unloaded. Our ship was then bound for Liverpool. Our course was straight across the Channel and then down the English coast. We did not have a convoy but had a pilot onboard. It was in the afternoon when we left Boulogne, and that night we anchored in the roads off Portsmouth.

There were mine fields laid all along the coast, and I heard the pilot tell the captain that it was hard enough to get through it in the daylight without trying it at night. The daylight found us on our way and all were happy to know that in a couple of days at the longest, we should be in Liverpool with our pay and enjoying whatever Liverpool had to offer in the way of amusement.

Most of the crew lived in Liverpool, and it was only natural that they were anxious to see their sweethearts and wives. I would be a stranger but that did not bother me as I was at home in any port. I did not doubt that I could find a sweetheart without any trouble.

It was near two bells in the first dog watch and my watch below. I was in the washroom talking to some of the sailors who were washing their clothes in order to be all ready to land when we should reach port the next day, if we did not anchor that night again. We were interrupted by a bang, which sounded like someone had slammed a door. A tremble went through the ship and I could not think what had happened. Some of the other sailors knew as they had had some experiences in the danger zone. They very quickly let me know that we had been torpedoed. We all made a dash for our respective quarters and got our personal effects, which we had all ready for an emergency. I had all my money, papers and sailor permits which had been given to us as soon as we left Buenos Aires, in an oilskin bag under my shirt. I grabbed a jersey and my go-ashore coat and was on deck in a second. The mate was blowing his whistle to call all hands on deck. We mustered on the boat deck along side of our appointed lifeboats, as we had been instructed to do. There was not as much excitement as one would think. British seamen are noted for being very disorderly and awful growlers, but in an emergency they are very cool.

The ship was hit near the boiler room, and several of the men below were lost. One of our sailors had a young brother who was making his first trip to sea, as a coal passer. He was one of the missing. It was hard on the brother, and we felt sorry for him, as we knew that another brother had been killed in France. It would be a very sad homecoming for him.

The steam was rushing up from the engine and boiler room, so the order was given to launch the boats. My station was at one of the falls.[54] The boats were already swinging out board, the order to lower away was no more than given, and the falls were swinging through the blocks. Each boat crew was in their respective boats; the only ones left aboard were the men lowering away. As soon as the boats were in the water we would slide down the fall into the boat. Our boat crew was in such a hurry that as soon as the boat hit the water they pulled away. I climbed down to the saloon deck and dove off. The other sailor jumped from the boat deck. Oh Boy! The water was cold. It was only when the crew saw us in the water, that they came to their senses and realized that they had forgotten us. What we told them when they finally hauled

---

[54] The ropes used for lowering and raising the lifeboats.

us in, was a plenty. The crew tried to square themselves by offering us some of their dry clothing which we did not accept, as our clothes were better and as it looked like rain, we knew they would soon be as wet as we were. We did accept some of their tobacco and it was not long until we were joking about our bath. The ship did not sink as soon as we thought she would. It was fully an hour before she went down. We bade farewell to the *La Negro*. Houlder Bros. Lines had lost a fine ship. I lost a large part of my belongings and I learned that the least we have the least we can loose. As soon as our ship had been torpedoed, the wireless operator sent out an SOS. The *La Negro* had hardly sunk when we sighted a vessel's smoke heading our way. A British Patrol boat had picked up our SOS. It did not make directly for us as I had expected, but made a large circle around, gradually drawing closer to us. It was scouting for the submarine before picking us up. If the submarine was still in the vicinity, the patrol boat was not taking any chances of being torpedoed. The submarine had evidently made for deep water as soon as it had torpedoed us. It would lie on the bottom of the sea and wait in safety until dark, when it could carry on its work of destruction under cover of the darkness. I was wishing that the patrol boat could find it and destroy it.

When the patrol boat did stop to pick us up, it made a quick job of it. It hardly slackened speed until abreast of us, when its engines were put full astern, and we were very unceremoniously hauled aboard and were under way, full speed ahead, steering a zigzag course for Plymouth.

We were given some rum, food, and cocoa that had a quarter of inch of fat on it. The two of us who were wet, soon had clothing drying around the boiler tops, and when we reached Plymouth, we were once more in dry clothing. Before I had time to realize it, we were ashore and rushed aboard a train for Liverpool. I was in a third class compartment that was very crowded and I had quite a time to get comfortable. It was a great relief to get out at the different stations and stretch my legs. Traveling third class in England is worse than riding in a boxcar in the States.

It was late the next afternoon when we reached Liverpool. There we separated. The men who had homes headed to them, and we who did not headed to the South Side Sailors' Home. The other sailor who got wet when leaving the *La Negro* had no relatives in Liverpool, and as it was my first visit, he led the way to the Sailors' Home. We were lucky enough to get a room. We decided that the first thing was to get some new clothing. As he did not get paid until the next day, I loaned him money. We were soon dressed and ready to go.

Chapter 12
Fire and Topedoes

I have made many visits to England, but I never could keep track of the time of their meals. You are supposed to eat five times a day, and I was lucky if I could be on time for three. Part of the time I got in on the fourth meal. I have no complaint to make of the quantity of meals, but the quality of the food that I was served was not only poor but there was very little of it. At my first meal in the Sailors' Home, what I took to be a very liberal helping of cheese, turned out to be bread. War bread, they called it and I give them credit for naming it correctly, as it would make any man want to fight. As I had to pay the same whether I had my meals or not, I ate dinner, which was a fairly passable meal at the Sailors' Home. The rest of my meals I took in restaurants. In the restaurants, I was again reminded of the war. I wished for ham and eggs, but I would have to eat the ham in one restaurant and the eggs in another, or visa versa, as they never served them together. There were meatless days. I don't know how they expected to win the war by going half starved. There was one advantage caused by the war. The pubs were opened in the morning for a couple of hours and then closed until evening. One could get drunk in the morning, go to bed, and be sober in time for their opening in the evening. Before the war, a man had to be satisfied with one drunk a day.

The actions of some of the many countrymen of mine, who were in Liverpool on their way to the front, attracted my attention. I wondered if, when they signed up to go to war, they realized it was to fight the Germans not their Allies. Also, if they realized that the war of 1812 was over, and that we were at peace with England, in fact one of our allies.

Every night there was a fight between some American and English soldiers. At the American Bar on Lime St., there was always trouble between the soldiers. I figured that my countrymen were in such a hurry to get into the war that they were taking that way of getting in trim; thus when they met the Germans, they could wade right through them.

I had heard a great deal about the good times to be had in Merry England, but I could not see anything very merry there. There were too many restrictions, and the price of everything was double or triple the pre-war prices. I decided to make my stay short. I started to look for a ship, and it did not take long to find one. I signed on a ship belonging to what the sailors called the Maggie Booth Line. I did not know as much about the outfit then as I do now, or I should never have signed on. Luck was with me once more. The Kaiser, for once, did me a good turn.

The ship was bound for Brazil only partly loaded with general cargo. The second day out from Liverpool, the Kaiser cut our trip short by slipping a torpedo into the worst bundle of starvation in the way of a ship afloat. We were somewhere in the vicinity of the Scilly Islands. A Penzance fishing boat picked us up. All hands were saved. The boat landed us at the old fishing port of Penzance, and once more, I was railroaded to Liverpool. Instead of a long sea voyage on a hungry ship, I received a month's pay for two days' work. I lost no time in getting another ship. That time I used better judgment and signed on the *El Uruguay*. That was another ship for frozen meats and owned by the Houlder Bros. Line. We were bound for Buenos Aires, which pleased me. Once more, I was sailing away from Merry England bound for the Rio Plata. That trip we were fortunate; we did not come in contact with a submarine.

The *El Uruguay* was good for sixteen knots, so we were very soon out of the danger zone and into the balmy tropics. The ship had a six-inch gun mounted on the poop deck. It furnished us a bit of amusement. Several of the sailors were detailed for the gun's crew. Three navy men handled the

143

gun and the rest, me one of them, passed the ammunition. My station was between decks, where with the help of an old Irishman, we hoisted the ammunition out of the lazaret.[55] When gun practice was over we lowered the ammunition down into the lazaret. The cases were heavy and we used a handy billy or light block and tackle.

I will never forget the first time we had gun practice. The carpenter had rigged up a target with barrels and planks lashed together which was lowered into the water and allowed to drift astern. The Irishman and I were sent to our station, and from where we were, we could not see what was going on up on the deck. While we were busy hoisting up cases of ammunition, we could hear the mate, who was at the range finder, calling out 500, 1000, 1500, and so on. One of the men at the gun was repeating the distances, when all of a sudden, just as we set a case down, bang, they fired the gun. My first thought was that the case of ammunition had exploded. It was my first experience being near a six inch gun when it was fired. We were directly under the gun, down in the ship's hold; therefore, we received the full shock and our share of the noise. It felt as if the ship had blown to pieces. My eardrums rang for a day and I could not hear very well. My Irish partner did not wait for them to fire a second time. He climbed out of the hold and ran for the fo'c'sle screaming, "My ears are busted, my ears are busted. I am ruined for life. I can't hear a thing. I shipped on this ship as a sailor and I will have no more to do with your damn gun." And he did not. The mate ordered him to go back to his station, and the answer that Paddy gave him was, "I can't hear a word you say. I'm ruined for life." The captain tried, but he did not have any success. The mate threatened to log him, have him up for refusing duty, and everything else that can be done to a sailor in like circumstances, but not a budge could he get out of Paddy, beyond, "I can't hear a word you say. I'm ruined for life."

---

[55] A storeroom near a vessel's stern.

Paddy never went near the gun again. The captain did not bother him about the gun anymore, nor did he log him for refusing duty. Paddy was over sixty years old and a good sailor, a very fine old man to get along with, but as he said himself, a damn poor man around a gun. Paddy's behavior gave us many hearty laughs.

We had two gun practices going out. They fired three shots each time. After the first shot, I did not mind it so much, although I can't say that I ever learned to like it. The ship stopped at Dakar on the West Coast of Africa. There we left the gun, as we could not enter Buenos Aires, a neutral port, with a gun mounted. At Dakar, our ship laid out at anchor. A barge came alongside to take the gun and ammunition. Aboard the barge were both men and women. Some of the women had babies with them. I shall never forget the women and the babies. The women's dresses consisted of a piece of cloth wrapped around their waists, one end hanging down to form the skirt, the other end was thrown over their shoulders leaving both breasts exposed. Such breasts, they hung down to the waist. The babies were tucked into the cloth that was across the shoulders and back. What was so astonishing to me was that when some of the babies wanted to be fed, the mother just took the breast and chucked it (yes, chucked is the right word) up over her shoulder and the baby grabbed it like a young terrier would a bone. When the milk was gone out of one, the mother would very unceremoniously pass up the other and this I noticed as a rule put the baby to sleep. When upon being released by the young savage, the breast dropped back to the front of its own accord. These natives can never be accused of any false modesty.

Our stay at Dakar was but a few short hours, and I must say amusing ones. We were on our way again with only the regular work of the ship to bother us. In due time, we were making our ship fast in Dique Norte in Buenos Aires.

My day's work was over and I was soon ashore having a good time. The unrestricted ways of Buenos Aires were a pleasure after the red tape of England and France. To be able to sit down in a café and order what one wished to eat or drink was a joy indeed. The only thing asked was to have money to pay for what was ordered.

We had to work hard during the day to get the ship ready for her cargo of meat. As soon as the cargo was out of each compartment, we would clean it and rig up the freezing coils. When the entire cargo was out, we had our first easy time of this trip, while waiting for the ship's hold to cool off. It had to be thoroughly cooled before the meat could be loaded. We took on only part of our cargo at Buenos Aires and as before went to Ensenada for the rest.

We had quite a little fun in Ensenada. The mate put us to painting the funnels of the ship while the meat was being loaded. The ship was docked along side of a building where many girls were working. From our position on the funnels, we were able to talk with the girls and it was not long until there was more flirting going on than work. The floor lady in the factory was having her troubles trying to keep the girls at work. The mate did not bother us, as I think he was having as much fun as we were. Our foolishness had been going on for about an hour, when a very officious looking Englishman came aboard and asked for the captain or the chief officer. The man on the gangway pointed out the mate, whom the Englishman quickly approached and informed that he was the superintendent of the department where the girls were working, and that the mate must stop us from bothering the girls. They were neglecting their work, and he did not want anymore of that damn foolishness. The mate stood for a moment sizing him up from head to foot and then said, "You keep your girls from the windows, stop them from bothering my men, and my men will not bother them. Your girls have interfered enough. That funnel should have been finished by now, and look, they are not a third through. The fault of it all, is that you have no discipline in your factory." The mate left the superintendent standing there very much amazed. He must have thought that the mate would raise the devil with us. He went back to the factory but I know that he did not have much success keeping the girls at work as they were at the windows until we finished and that was at noon.

They finished loading the ship in the afternoon and we were on our way again. We made a stop in Montevideo for a few hours. We took on coal and another gun. We sailors thought that we might stop at Dakar and take on the gun we had left, but every movement of the ship was kept a secret. The crew never knew what the next move would be. We knew that we would have to make a call at some port for coal before we could reach France or England, as we had only loaded on a few hundred tons at Montevideo. Why we did not take on more, I do not know as we had sailed with our bunkers only partly filled.

The ship was just six hours out of Montevideo when fire was discovered in the coalbunkers. The ship was headed back to Montevideo and all hands were put to work to fight the fire, which is the most dreaded thing at sea. The smoke was pouring out of the bunker hatches and ventilators in the boiler room. The plates in the bulkhead were very hot. Water was turned in through the hatches but it did not seem to do any good. They then bored some holes through the bulkhead plates in the boiler room, large enough to get the nozzle of the hose through. In this way, the fire was kept in check until we reached Montevideo, where the coal was unloaded. Oily waste rags, or something that had caused spontaneous combustion probably caused the fire. We blamed some German or German sympathizer among the stevedores who had loaded the coal. We were in port two days getting the coal out and more in. The coal that we took that time was very thoroughly inspected for anything that might cause fire. The Germans got a good cussing from all hands. The fire did no damage to the ship beyond the delay, but we did not enjoy the extra work, and it surely put a crimp in our dispositions. We did not know what trouble to expect next.

After a few days at sea, we forgot all about the fire and were looking ahead to the near future when we should again be in the danger zone. The voyage between Europe and the Rio Plata always appealed to me as there is not much cold weather to bother. I always enjoyed the tropics, where I could roll my bedding out on the deck and lie there wondering what all the stars and planets in the heavens are; whether they are inhabited and if so, what the inhabitants do; if they have seas with ships sailing on them, and if so, are the sailors as carefree as these on earth, or if they had wars with submarines and mines to bother them. With such thoughts, I would drop off to sleep, such as can only be enjoyed after work in the open air. All too quickly, it seemed but a few minutes (actually three hours), I would be awakened to go on watch for four hours.

The trip through the tropics passed all too quickly, with a stop at St. Vincent, Cape Verde Island for bunkers. All too soon, we were back in the danger zone, and in a few days we reached the south of the English Channel. We did not see any submarines but had a good scare. Over the wireless, we received a message that submarines were in our vicinity. Orders were given for all speed possible, and the engine room crew sure responded. Our regular speed of sixteen knots was increased to over twenty-two, if the reports that reached us sailors were correct. Whatever the speed, the ship vibrated so badly that I expected to see the mast snap in two. To make things still more interesting, all hands, cook, steward, and everyone available were put on lookout, stationed at every place of any advantage. My station was on the main mast and it was all that I could do to keep from being shaken off. I know that if I had had false teeth I could not have kept them in. The sensation was awful. I felt as if every bone in my body would be shaken loose and a miracle that they were not. We sighted lots of wreckage, barrels, water casks, cases, and many different parts of ships that had fallen prey to the enemy. A grim reminder of what our fate at any moment might be, a corpse would bob up, making us shudder; hence helping to feed our hatred for the enemy.

After a few hours of this mad sailing, we sighted land - France - and not any too soon to suit me. We were sailing into the harbor at Brest. Oh! How good it felt to be safe once more. We lay out at anchor, to wait for a convoy as on our previous visit. It was very interesting just to look around at the different vessels anchored about us in the harbor. The old city of Brest snuggled together at the head of the bay. The farms in the distant hills, with their whitewashed building and stone walls, had a look of endurance and age. I should have enjoyed taking a ramble through the hills. I could also imagine how good a big glass of milk from one of the many cows grazing on the green hillsides would taste with some fresh baked bread from the farmhouse. It seems that aboard a British ship a sailor's one big wish is for something good to eat. Better shipmates or finer officers to be with would be hard to find, but the cooks are poor. For a nation that likes good food, the British flag flies over more rotten cooks than any other flag in the world. If they have any good cooks, it has never been my good fortune to sample their work.

We had to wait until the next day before enough ships were gathered there to make up the convoy. Three destroyers escorted us, but we sailors were on the lookout the entire time. We stopped at Cherbourg and Havre. The reason for stopping, I never learned. The submarines were very active and sinking a great many ships. I suppose that had something to do with our staying for hours at the different ports. The commander of the convoy was using all care possible to get us safely into the harbor of Boulogne. As the convoys were transports carrying cargo, it was very important to get the food and other materials for the war through safely.

There was plenty to remind us of the war. Wreckage was drifting in all directions, ship masts were sticking above the water showing where a ship had met a submarine or run into a mine. Good luck was with us, for we neither met a submarine nor did we run into a mine, and reached Boulogne safely late in the afternoon.

Shore leave and passes were issued to all hands as soon as the ship was made fast. I took immediate advantage of my pass and went directly to a little café I had found when there before, and soon had a good meal and a bottle of wine before me. While there seemed to be a shortage of food in England, in France I did not have any trouble in getting whatever I wanted, as long as I had the money to pay for it. The French are not at all backward in charging and their hands are out for more money with regularity equal to that of a circus elephant's trunk reaching for peanuts. Somehow, I never found it hard to pass over the francs when a pretty little mademoiselle was asking for them.

We stayed in Boulogne about two weeks and there was plenty of excitement. There were air raids at night and there was a rumor out that the Germans were going to drop poison gas, but it never materialized while we were there; however, it had us guessing.

There was a continuous line of ambulances bringing the wounded down from the front to be loaded on the hospital ships bound for England. By the number of wounded that were being brought down, we knew that there was heavy fighting going on at the front. All of the soldiers that I talked with were very doubtful as to how the war would end. But whichever way it was to be, they would be glad to see it finished.

We sailed from Boulogne on a morning's tide for Liverpool which we reached in due time without any trouble. We were all paid off and were soon gone on our many ways. I stayed at the South Side Sailors' Home as I wanted to save my money. My stay in Liverpool was not very exciting. After a few days' rest, I started out to find a ship, and I had no trouble finding one. I joined the *El Paraguay*, the same ship that I had recently left. According to the superstition of the sailors, it is bad luck to make two trips in succession on the same ship, or to go to sea with money in one's pocket. Throwing all precaution to the wind, I signed on and once more was on my way to Buenos Aires. We had no trouble in getting through the danger zone, and it was a great relief because we did not know what minute we might be blown to Kingdom Come.

There was one big trouble that we could not leave behind and that was poor food. The steward for some reason had a grudge against the sailors and was taking it out on us by starving us. The firemen and sailors were supposed to get the same food, but we did not. The firemen were well fed, while we sailors were getting wet hash three times a day. There was lots of discontent and plenty of complaints made to the steward and the captain, but it did no good. I knew that it would do no good to go aft, that is to the captain or steward. I was waiting until we reached port before I did any growling. I did not care to get into trouble on the high sea, especially, as I knew that I would get no satisfaction from it.

The sailors were a very heterogeneous lot. Some were boys from a reformatory ship, and they were little devils. They would have stolen the ship's anchor if it had not been fastened to the ship with a chain. Tobacco, matches, or clothing would very mysteriously disappear, never to return. The only thing that was safe was soap. They would never bother that. Among the men, there were only four or five with any experience, the rest were just pick-ups. We had one barber, another was deaf, and an old Irishman who had been on fishing vessels all his life. They were not bad fellows to get along with, but as they did not know their work, it made it bad for us who did. We had to do more than our share. The war had caused such a demand for seamen that they were glad to man the ships with whomsoever they could get. He that could or would work had to make up for what the others lacked. With poor shipmates and worse food, the trip was not as pleasant as it might have been. It was a welcome morning to me when we made fast to the dock in Buenos Aires.

We arrived at Buenos Aires shortly after daylight, and as soon as the ship was fast, we knocked off for breakfast. I had been on watch since twelve o'clock midnight, and when I went below for breakfast I was not in a very good humor. When I saw the ever-present wet hash, which looked wetter than usual, it was like waving a red flag before an enraged bull. I grabbed up the mess kit and carried it to the captain, who was standing on the saloon deck. I told him that we wanted something fit to eat and that hash had been our diet ever since the ship had left Liverpool. He called the steward and told him what I had said. The steward told the captain that I was nothing but a sea lawyer and an agitator, and that we had been fed extra well, and to prove it he fetched a menu he had. From which he read what we were supposed to have had each day. It sure sounded fine, and it made my mouth water. This fateful morning, we were to have had curry stew.

"Look!" the steward said to the captain, "All the nice meat and vegetables." When he said nice meat and vegetables, something snapped in me, and I slammed the slimy conglomeration, mess kit and all, right into the steward's face. I made a ringer. The mess kit caught him fair and square. I left it hanging on his head and uniform. I was not long in deciding that that ship was no place for me, and that I had better make myself scarce. I made a hasty retreat to the other side of the ship, which was the side next to the dock and rushed the gangway. I was soon lost among the crowd along the dock. From the corner of a warehouse, I could see a very much bespattered and enraged captain and steward looking up and down the docks for me, but in my hiding place I was invisible to them.

Their appearance soon drew a crowd along the side of the ship. Neither the captain nor the steward could speak Spanish. They were making wild gestures at the crowd. As there was some danger of someone in the crowd understanding them,

I decided to move while moving was good. It took only a few minutes for me to put two blocks between the ship and me. I caught a streetcar which took me to the Boca at the other end of the city. I went to a small café on a side street where I had stayed before. I knew that I would be safe there until the ship sailed again. I did not want to be taken on the ship, as I knew that I would be dealt with very severely on the return to England.

All the clothes that I owned were those that I had on. The few that I had left aboard the ship were of little value. I had a little over five hundred pesos when I changed the English money that I had into South American money. The exchange was low as the British paper money was looked on with suspicion. My discharge papers I had in a small bag around my neck. My passport was in the captain's possession. He had taken it just before the ship entered Buenos Aires. It did not worry me then, but caused a lot of trouble and inconvenience later.

My thoughts were on consuming some civilized food. I ordered lamb chops, fried eggs, hot rolls, and a quart bottle of beer. I was soon in a good humor. I then told my friends about my morning fracas. They were all very much amused and sympathized with me. They wanted me to lie in wait that night for the captain and the steward and throw one or both of them into the docks. My grudge was not quite that deep. I did not blame the captain as much as I did the steward. The captain had lots of troubles and worries, but I sure would like to have had a battle with that steward, but we never met again. That was the last British ship that I ever sailed on, and I am not anxious to go on another, not even as a passenger.

As I had plenty of money for the time, I did not worry about ships. I bought a few clothes and then settled down to enjoy life for a while. It was probably a month before I discovered that my finances were getting low and that I had better be looking for another ship. There is where my troubles began.

There were plenty of ships and many of them wanted sailors but not me. I did not have a passport, nor would the Council give me one. I was not long in finding that I was out of luck as far as getting a ship was concerned. I managed to get a few days' work on ships that were laying in port for repairs. When it came to signing on, no, I could not make it. I was getting desperate. My money was gone and I was just making enough to pay my board. I did not have enough clothes to make a flying jib for a wheelbarrow. Buenos Aires is like all cities - fine if you have plenty of money, but not so good when you are short of money.

I soon realized that I would have to do something quickly. I could have gone back to my job on the ranch at Santa Cruz, but I did not, as I did not like to acknowledge being defeated. My prospects for the future did not look very good. I hunted the waterfront day after day, glad to pick up whatever work I could. There were many others in the same fix as me; likewise a great many Germans who could not even get work on the neutral ships.

There was another species of humanity that would always remind a fellow to be on his guard, or Buenos Aires and her winning ways would get him: the beachcombers - and there were plenty of them. A more degenerated white man it would be hard to imagine. They have not one bit of self respect left. Dirty, barefooted, and many with no other clothing except a pair of ragged pants.

The surprising thing about them is that most of them have come down from the higher stations of life. There was one German about fifty years old, who had held a very high position in a German Argentina Banking Company. The nightlife got him, and many more like him: English, German, and Scandinavian. I never ran across any Americans, although there may have been some. These men came out to Argentina to fill good positions. Women and drink got them. They lost their positions and gradually sank lower and lower, until their only ambition in life was a bottle of cheap wine, which was made from dye, wood, and alcohol. For their food, whatever scraps they could pick up around the docks seemed to satisfy them. They were like animals. There was only one good thing about them—they served as a good warning to others. I have heard many of the sailors say, "Watch out, don't get on the beach in Buenos Aires," and it is very seldom that a sailor ever does.

The Buenos Aires police receive their pay from the fines of those they arrest. As there is no chance of getting any money from the beachcombers, they were never molested.

The white slave trade flourished in Buenos Aires, and there were hundreds of brothels. There were only two women (old hags) on the beach. One of them was called Irish Mary. She was the nearest thing to a moving Egyptian mummy that you could imagine. Just yellow like parchment and just hide stretched over a skeleton. She was such a pitiable sight that many gave her a few coins to get her out of their sight. But like an alley cat, she had her friends. I was told that shortly before I was there, that she gave birth to a baby in the Salvation Army Quarters. She discarded the child and was back on the beach in ten days. The other woman's story I never learned.

There was a hoard of beggars, little girls between the ages of five and eleven. It seems that when they reach the age of ten or eleven that they disappear, probably to enter one of the many brothels at a more profitable occupation. One would think that with so many brothels, when the women lost their attractiveness with age, there would be many more of them on the beach. But it was common talk in Buenos Aires, when they could bring in no more money to their exploiters, that they were taken for a boat ride, and they did not return. How much truth there was in that I do not know. The waterfront of Buenos Aires was a close second to what the waterfront of San Francisco was before the earthquake.

Crimps (runners), for the seamen boarding houses, were ever ready to exact blood money from the sailors or captains. Many of these crimps worked in cahoots with the councils. It cost a sailor a month's wages to get a ship, and if men were scarce, the captain would have to pay too. These crimps are just a bunch of parasites of the lowest type and to think that the councils (men sent to represent their respective countries) would work with them was appalling. The almighty dollar will cause men to do most anything.

A big Georgian Negro named Brown had the monopoly on American ships. Two white men acted as runners for him. A sailor had to be ever on his guard for there were many kinds of crooks always ready to fleece him of his last dollar, and like the crimps, ready to get the money before it was earned.

As for me, I did not intend to buy any job, not if I never got one. One day when I was rather downhearted, I began to think of Red, my outlaw friend. He was at least straight and above board, and he did not prey on those who had to work for their living. I wished that I had joined his band when I met him in Patagonia. He told me that if ever I changed my mind and wanted to join him that I would find him during the winter in a town in Bolivia, as they stayed in this town when not on the road. The more I thought about it the more anxious I was to go. I had made up my mind that if I did not get a ship within another ten days that I would beat my way to Bolivia and see if I could find Red. If a little piece of paper with my photo on it was going to keep me from working, I would turn outlaw and live anyway. This I had settled in my mind.

Chapter 13
Sailing: Hot to Cold

At last my luck changed. The next day after I had decided to turn outlaw, I got work on a Danish ship – the *Neils R. Finsen.* I had been working two days when I got a chance to talk with the captain. He was a fine old gentleman and very friendly. I told him that I wanted to get to the States. I also told him of the predicament that I was in and asked if I could get to the States, would he be able to fix things for me. The next day he called me to his room. He told me to go to my council and they would give me a permit to go to the States. Boy! Was I happy. I forgot all about becoming an outlaw. I went to the council and sure enough I got the permit.

After signing on that ship, I went ashore with some of the sailors. We were in a café called the Nelson Bar. I picked up an acquaintance with an Englishman, and in our talk I learned that he had just come from Bolivia. I asked him if he had met any Americans up there. He said, yes, there were a few, but most of the foreigners were German. He told me that an American outlaw was killed just before he had left Bolivia. He said that the outlaw was called Rubio. The description that he gave me was Red's. The Englishman had not seen the outlaw himself but had talked with others who had. From what he told me, I was sure it was Red who had been killed. Well, it is one occupation where one is likely to die with his boots on. It seems that Red had taken some new members into the band, and there was a dispute as to who was going to be the boss. The result was Red's death, also the death of several of the others of the band, and some were badly wounded. That finished a band of much-wanted outlaws. I felt very sorry for

Red, as there was much that we had in common. Montana, Nevada, Patagonia, and all the other range country that we had rambled over. In some way I felt that not only had I seen the last of Red, but also the last of the life we both knew.

The day for the ship to sail arrived. I had been in and around Buenos Aires for three months and had seen many ups and downs. I was glad to get away and to be headed for God's country. I had been away a long time and I knew that I would find many changes. The ship was bound for Boston, loaded with wool and hides. My shipmates were all Scandinavians except one, an Argentine. All could speak English but the Argentine. He caused lots of fun for us because the mate could speak to him only in sign language.

We had aboard a coop of chickens. Part of the work assigned to the Argentine was the cleaning every day of the chicken coop. When the mate wanted him to clean the coop, he would flap his arms up and down, shuffle his feet on the deck, and crow like a rooster. The Argentine would then understand him. We enjoyed it very much as the mate was an elderly man and nearly six feet tall. We looked forward each day for the show.

We were a very happy crowd and all got along nicely together. As I was the only one that could speak a little Spanish, the Argentine leaned on me a great deal.

The food was exceptionally good, barring breakfast. We had the same thing every morning, coffee, bread, potatoes, and raw salt herring. The raw herring was what got the Argentine and me. It was something that neither of us was accustomed to. The Argentine asked me if the Danish were salvajes, that is savages. I told him that raw herring was one of the favorite items of food in their country, and that outside of that they lived the same as other people. I was accustomed to many different foods, and made up my mind that as long as they were good, and the others could eat them, so could I. The Argentine did likewise and we soon learned to like the raw salt herring. The rest of our meals were fine, and the best that I had on any ship. The officers were very good to work under, so our trip north was like a trip would have been on a yacht, compared to what my former ships had been.

The *Neils R. Finsen* was a very old style ship. There was not any wheelhouse, just an open bridge. While it was very nice in the warm weather, when we got farther north and got into the cold weather it was not so nice. It was summer when we left Buenos Aires and winter when we arrived in Boston. I will never forget the morning we took aboard a pilot at Martha's Vineyard. A cold north wind was blowing, and the water was covered with slush ice. When the pilot came up on the bridge, the captain went below to breakfast. I had just come to the wheel. I had the 8 a.m. to 10 a.m. wheel. I had on all the clothes that I owned and that was not much. What I had was made to wear in the tropical countries. For those that do not know, Nantucket Sound is not very tropical in the month of February (1918). The pilot had on a big fur coat, fur mittens, and overshoes. I had on a light coat, a cap that I could not pull down over my ears, no mittens or overshoes, and thin cotton underwear. The pilot asked me if I understood English. I told him that was the only language that I could speak anyway near intelligently. He asked, "Ain't you a Dane?" I replied, "I am an American." He said, "What in the hell are you doing on this old tub with no wheel house?" I replied, "This is not an old tub but a real sea going yacht." The pilot said, "I am glad that I can't be arrested for having a different opinion."

"Are you cold?" he asked. "Cold," I said, "You don't call this cold do you? Excuse me I forgot that you are used to being coddled in a steam-heated wheelhouse and are not used to a real man's ship. I am not cold, and I am enjoying this nice cool, embracing weather immensely." If I had never told a lie before, I sure was making up for lost time. I was so cold that I was afraid to move quickly for fear that I would snap in two. When I was relieved at four bells, I made a beeline for the fire room gratings, where it took me the best part of the next two hours of my watch to get thawed out. As there was not any fire in the fo'c'sle, the boiler room was the only place where we sailors could go to get warm. When we went below, it was to eat and then climb into our bunks and cover up and try to keep warm. It was very disagreeable, but after all, I felt lucky to be where I was. I had three more turns at the wheel before we docked in Boston. I was sure glad when we were made fast. As soon as we passed the doctor's examination and our papers were examined, we drew our money and went ashore. I made a beeline to a clothing store, Talberts, and invested in some clothes that were made from that fleecy stuff that grows on a sheep's back. I sure got a setback when I found what the war time prices were. Two flannel shirts that cost $2.50 or $3.00 pre-war prices, cost $6.00 apiece, two heavy suits of underwear, socks, and a pair of trousers, and the $50.00 that I had drawn was shot. I was happy just the same. I decided to stay with the ship, as I did not have but very little money coming to me, besides not knowing what trouble I would have in getting a passport. Furthermore, the ship was bound for New York, from Boston so I would go that far and build my plans accordingly.

My first impression of Boston was not a very good one. The weather was anything but pleasant. Worst of all were the streets. The man who laid out the streets was either an ex- cowpuncher or a maniac. The streets reminded me of a number of cow trails leading to a water hole. Boston Commons and Skully Square represented the water holes. If I started out to go up around Boston Commons, I was sure to land at Skully Square and vice versa. Anyone, who would spend two or three weeks in Boston and not get lost, would be qualified to go to darkest Africa or to the Polar Regions and not be afraid of getting lost. The only reason that Boston has not produced more explorers is that they cannot find their way out of the city.

Another thing that interested me was the neat little graveyards that they have along the main street. By the dates on the headstones, some of the graves contain the remains of some of the deck hands off the Mayflower. There are names on many of the headstones that I have a faint memory of from days gone by, when schoolteachers had tried to impress upon me the importance of those who had figured in our early American history. Some of the buildings looked old enough to tell some very interesting tales if it were possible for them to speak. There are many interesting places to see in Boston, but I had neither the money nor the time to see many of them.

It took only a few days to discharge our cargo, and we were steaming down the coast to New York. Before daylight on a cold and extremely dark morning we were in the lower bay, where we took aboard a pilot, who took the ship into New York. We dropped anchor in the upper bay for quarantine. The doctor and port officials came aboard. They did not detain us long, and we were soon on our way through the traffic of New York Harbor. What a sight it was! Ferry boats flying here and there, tug boats, and many other different crafts that you will find in the busiest ports of the world.

My turn at the wheel came after we passed inspection. I do not know of a more thrilling experience than steering a ship through the heavy traffic of New York Harbor. The temperature was below zero. Pancake ice floating by would grate on the ship's sides, causing a weird sound. We would just clear a big car float by a few feet, then a saucy little tug would steam across our bow. Next, a side-wheeler passenger ferry with its load of early morning workers would just clear us by what seemed a dangerously small margin. The pilot never spoke a word, just a slight motion of his hand to port or starboard. It was sure a relief to be with a man who could handle a ship with such ease going through such heavy traffic, and without speaking, be able to guide the ship safely through.

The glances that I stole, to first one side and then the other, had me wondering what the different places were that we were passing. It was my first trip to New York. Naturally, I was very curious. I had heard a great deal about the city, and I was trying to identify some of the things and places, but I could only guess at them, and found later that most of my guesses were wrong. The Statue of Liberty was about the only thing that I guessed correctly. Soon after passing the Statue of Liberty, we docked at the Munson Line docks, and in a few hours, we were loading general cargo for Cuba.

When we sailors learned that the ship was bound for Cuba, we decided to go. The captain told us that we would be paid the American scale of wages, which was higher than what we had signed on for in Buenos Aires. He was very much pleased that we were staying, as men were scarce and hard to get.

Some of the other sailors had been in New York before and knew the ropes. Several of us decided that we would get a room in the Seamen's Institute on South Street, which was only a block from the ship, and would be warmer than our quarters in the fo'c'sle of the ship. The Sailors' Home, as seamen referred to it, is the most wonderful institute of its kind in the world. Only a very small charge is made, and one receives many an accommodation that would be impossible for a seaman with small wages to afford. A single room, warm and clean, cost thirty-five cents. Large shower baths, which would be hard to find in many of the large hotels, are located on every floor. The water was always hot, and there was plenty of it. I for one certainly enjoyed the shower baths and did justice to them by having a shower before turning in and another when I turned out in the morning.

There is a large auditorium in the building, and every night there was an entertainment of some kind. Large reading rooms with plenty of papers, books, and magazines were there also. As I had not had much of an opportunity for a few years to read, I took full advantage of it. It was a big time for me just to sit in a comfortable chair and try to catch up with what my country had been doing in the years that I had been away. It was hard to realize that such a change could come about in such a short time. Ships were being built by the hundreds and in such a remarkable short time. Some were 90-day and some 30-day ships. Eagle boats and many other names that were all Greek to me. This made me feel as if I were Rip Van Winkle, the second. I began to realize how much I had wandered from the beaten paths of civilization. I knew that America had the name for doing things big and fast, but now it was bigger and faster. I was dazed by it all. The three nights that I had to spend reading just began to give me an idea of what was going on. I was very anxious to get into the whirl with the rest, but as I had very little money and only a few clothes, I could not take the chance of getting a ship across. The cold weather and I were not on the best of terms at that time and to cross the North Atlantic in the winter was no fun. I would have to buy more clothes and did not have the money, so on the fourth day I sailed with the *Neils R. Fensen* for Cuba.

In a couple of days, we were in the Gulf Stream and warmer weather. It was a big change. The ship was once more a comfortable place, everyone seemed more normal, and cold weather was all forgotten. It was just one of the many inconveniences that spring up in a sailor's life which are quickly forgotten. We had fine weather all the way down and although our ship was very slow, we made a good run, and all too soon for many of us we docked at Matanzas. Where we found New York too cold, Matanzas was too hot. It did not take long for me to see that Cuba had no color line. Negroes and whites were mingling together as one. Although I come from the North and did not draw the color line as close as do my countrymen of the Southern States, I did not like the way the whites and blacks mingled together in Cuba. I was not long in learning that the Cubans do not have much love for the Americans.

163

The mate was trying to get the boss stevedore to get his men to move faster. The boss stevedore told the mate that he could get no damn American style there and that the Danes were getting as bad as the Americans—all the time hurry up. He also said that the Cubans were not animals to be driven to suit any damn gringo.

Matanzas lies at the head of a long bay. It has a population of nearly fifty thousand. It is a very old city, and like most cities of Spanish origin, it has a very tragic history. The name Matanzas means slaughter, and many bloody battles have been fought in and near the city. On the road that we took from the dock to the city stands an old fort or citadel. It is very old, having been built in the early days by the Spanish settlers. I could not get much information from the natives, except that it was very old, and that many men had been tortured and put to death behind the grim stone walls of the fort. At the time I was there, the fort was used for barracks for the Cuban soldiers. These soldiers dressed very much as our doughboys do: stiff brim hats, khaki uniforms, many of which had faded until they were almost white. Matanzas has one of the largest universities in Cuba and is, therefore, one of the important seats of learning. There are many pretty homes, and of course, like all Spanish cities, it has beautiful plazas, statues, churches, and government buildings.

The Argentine and I spent our evenings rambling around, trying to see what we could. We did not have much time, as after our work was finished we had only two hours of daylight, but we made good use of the time.

Sugar was once more king in Cuba. There were signs of prosperity everywhere. The cafes were full of natives and money being spent very freely. Automobiles loaded with Whites and Negroes from the countryside would come speeding into town. They would be hanging on to every conceivable place possible to ride. A five-passenger car would be carrying ten or twelve people. Whether the road was smooth or rough did not make any difference in their speed; they all seemed happy and enjoying life. We docked on Monday. I fully expected to be in Matanzas over Sunday, so the Argentine and I had planned to visit some large stalactite caves, which are located about four miles from the city. We were very much disappointed. On Saturday we sailed for Cardenas, having taken on only a part of our cargo of sugar at Matanzas.

Sunday morning found us at anchor off Cardenas. There was no going ashore, as the water was not deep enough for our ship to go alongside the docks. Our cargo was brought out to us in lighters, and it made very slow work of the loading. The latter part of the week we sailed for Calbarien to finish loading. We also had to lay out at anchor there. If there is anything that will make a sailor madder than laying out at anchor and not being able to go ashore, I have so far failed to find it.

At last, the final sack of sugar was loaded and we battened down the hatches, and were steaming back to the U.S.A., with Galveston, Texas as our destination. We had rather expected to go north again, as there are large sugar refineries in Boston.

I had never been in Galveston, and it pleased me just as well, because I like to look over new places, and it would be warmer in Texas. It was but a few days until the ship was steaming over the bar and anchored in the Galveston Bay. We had to wait until the quarantine and other port officials gave the ship permission to dock. These officials did not waste any time, so we were soon tied up at the dock. All hand were paid off.

Chapter 14
Proving Citizenship

I was ready to face the customs officer and find out about getting a passport. I expected some trouble as my permit was just from Buenos Aires to the United States. I told the custom officer my trouble and was very much surprised when he said, "You write home and get yourself a birth certificate and in the meantime, you have two photographs taken." He gave me the address of the photographer to go to. It took but five or six days time and I was fixed up with a passport and draft registration card.

When the custom officer gave me my passport, he told me to go to the Charles Clark & Co., as they were badly in need of men for their tugboats. They were having trouble in keeping men. Tugboats and ships are very much different.

Sailors who have spent years on large ships may never know what it is to be seasick, but put them on a sea-going tug and they are like men who have never been to sea. I was very fortunate, as I never was sea sick on either ship or tug. When it came to sleeping, the more a vessel rolled the better I could sleep. Anyone who has ever been on tugs knows that they are noted for rolling.

The tugboat that I worked on towed barges of oil between the different ports along the Gulf of Mexico. In fine weather, like all ships, everything was fine, but it did not take very bad weather to make the tugs cut some funny capers. At times, getting over the Galveston bar would cause plenty of excitement. I have seen us ship seas that one would think a tug would never come from under. But a tug is built to withstand the bad weather. I remember one morning during breakfast we shipped a big sea, going over the Galveston bar. It came in through the door on the starboard side and washed all the food and dishes out through the door on the port side. It nearly drowned those of the crew who were eating their breakfast. The water was warm and after telling the man at the wheel what we thought of him, we took it as a joke. The cook could not see the joke as he had the mess to clean up and get more food ready.

OTTAWA STREET METHODIST EPISCOPAL CHURCH
WILLIAM A. FRYE, D. D. PASTOR
303 CASS STREET
TELEPHONE 895
JOLIET, - ILLINOIS

This certifies that William Lincoln, infant son of Thomas and Elizabeth Bakewell was baptized by The Rev. O.F.Mattison then Pastor of Ottawa St. Methodist Episcopal church in Joliet Illinois, April the twelfth eighteen hundred and eighty nine.

I hereby certify that the above is a correct copy of the records of the above mentioned Baptism as having taken place in the said Ottawa St. Methodist Episcopal Church.

Wm A. Frye

Now Pastor of said Church.

Dated Joliet Ill. This Fifth day of April Nineteen hundred and nineteen.

Letter from Ottawa Street Methodist Episcopal Church stating birth and baptism of Willam Lincoln Bakewell

I liked the life on a tug. It was free and easy. There was no discipline like there was on a large ship. The wages were good, and we had the best food. The time passed very quickly and before I realized it, the summer was gone and that glorious eleventh of November [1918] had come. The war was over and everyone was rejoicing.[56]

I had not intended to stay so long in and around Galveston, but I had made many friends and was happy and more contented than I had been for a long time. Finally, I made a change to a larger tug that was plying between the different American ports on the Gulf and Tampico, Mexico.

---

[56] Bakewell also spoke of being on a shrimp boat while writing for his proof of citizenship.

As the eighteenth amendment was being enforced, I knew that Mexico would be a little more interesting and offer more chance for excitement. I was right. Tampico was one wild place at that time as oil was king and lots of money was being made and being as freely spent. Like all oil boomtowns, Tampico had its share of riff raff followers. Robberies and murders were common things. He that earned his living by working had to be ever on the look out for the many that did not believe in work, and they were not all Mexicans.

Where we docked was four or five miles up the Panuco River from Tampico. It was a very lonesome road that we had to travel to get to town. Many a man was found along that road shot or stabbed to death. I had seen several. We never went into town alone. There were always five or six of us together, for we felt that there was strength in numbers. We were never bothered, and we traveled around Tampico and the road to the ship at all hours of the night. One morning a young American from another ship was found lying partly in the river. He had been killed by a number of knife wounds. I had had a drink with him the night before in a nearby canteen. He had bragged to us about how many greasers he had killed, and how many more that he was going to kill. It was very easy to see that he was looking for trouble. He was not disappointed.

There were a great many Mexicans from Texas in Tampico, and they were the worst, as they had it in for all Americans. If a man had sense enough to keep his mouth shut and mind his own business, there was not much trouble. Many of the gringos would get a few drinks under their belts and then become quarrelsome, and generally they would get the worst of the bargain.

The Gulf Refining Co., the owner of the tug that I was working on, had their own wharf, storehouses, and dwellings for their employees in Tampico. They kept a number of soldiers always on guard as they did not know what day a raid might be made.

VERIFICATIONS

SUBSEQUENT ARRIVALS IN THE UNITED STATES

POST	DATE	VESSEL	[SIGNATURE OF IMMIGRANT INSPECTOR]
Inc	23/7/19	EDGEFIELD	

SUBSEQUENT DEPARTURES FROM THE UNITED STATES

POST	DATE	VESSEL	[SIGNATURE OF CUSTOMS INSPECTOR]

Port of ...Galveston, Tex.,

...May 5, 1919, 19....

I, ...Fred C. Pabst.., ... Collector of the District of ...., do hereby certify that the person described on page 2 hereof has produced to me proof in the manner directed by law, and I do hereby certify that the said person is a citizen of the United States of America.

Permission is hereby granted the holder to depart from the port above mentioned.

This card must be verified by a Customs Inspector on each subsequent departure of the holder before he is permitted to sail.

In witness whereof I have hereunto set my hand and seal of office this .....5th..... day of .....May....., 19.....19.

Fred C. Pabst
(SEAL) .... *Collector of Customs.*

By .... Asst. Dep. Col.

The person described on page 2 hereof has been examined by me, and having produced satisfactory evidence of American citizenship, he is hereby granted permission to land.

This card must be verified by an Immigrant Inspector on each subsequent arrival of the holder before he is permitted to leave his vessel.

[SEAL.] .... *Immigrant Inspector,*

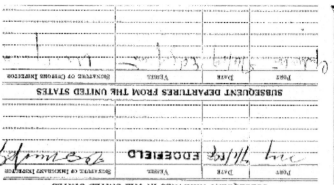

Port of ...Galveston, Tex.

NAME ....W. L. Bakewell,

Nationality ....American

Place of holder's birth .....Joliet, Ill.

Place of father's birth ......England.

Place of mother's birth .....Chicago, Ill.

If naturalized, where and when? ....

Age 50 or 11/26, is 18. Height ..5-5"

Vessel .Edgefield Flag ...Amer.

Date of arrival ...Apr. 24, 1919.

Description: Complexion Drk. Hair Dr.

Eyes ....Gray... Physical marks or peculiarities ....

William Bakewell's Citizen Seaman Identification Card

There is one night of my tugboat life that I will never forget. We were making a short trip with a barge load of oil from Lynchburg to Port Arthur, Texas. While crossing the Galveston Bay, a terrible electric storm came up; it was between eight and nine o'clock in the evening and darker than the proverbial black cat. The thunder rolled and the lightning flashed and cracked as I never remember seeing it do before or since. One minute it was so dark that we could not see the buoys that mark the narrow channel across the bay; then the next minute a flash of lightning would light up the whole bay.

The captain had decided to anchor the barge in the bay, and take the tug into Galveston for the night. When we arrived at the anchorage, we sighted another barge at anchor. While our captain was maneuvering our barge a safe distance from the other, we spied a light moving on the anchored barge. We thought it was a signal for us, and that someone on the barge wanted to go ashore. It was customary for the tugs to give men on an anchored barge a lift ashore, and that was what the captain intended to do, as soon as our barge was safely anchored. But, it was not to be as the captain had planned.

A flash of lightning lighted up the bay, and we could see a man on the barge, then we saw a streak of lightning strike the water a short distance from the barge. It ran along the water and struck the barge. A terrific explosion rent the air. It knocked us off our feet. From where the barge lay a few seconds before a tongue of flames rolled high into the Heavens. The black smoke high above reflected the light back. It was a very weird sight, more terrible than words can tell. There right before our eyes, men were being consumed in that terrible fire, and we were helpless to give them any aid. I doubt if there was any life left after the first explosion, as we did not see the bodies anywhere in the water. The barge went adrift soon after the explosion. Galveston missed one more terrible disaster. The wind was from the west. An east wind would have carried the burning barge up to the wharfs, burned a lot of the waterfront, and very likely many of the wooden buildings along it. The west wind carried the barge over to the east side of the bay, close to Port Bolivier, where it did no more damage. It burned all night and part of the next day.

It seems no matter how sad or terrible any disaster is, there is always a funny part and that one was no exception.

The weather was so bad the next day that we could not go on to Port Arthur. While we were tied to the wharf, a great many people came to inquire about the burning barge. Some of the questions asked, and some of the suggestions made were not only amusing but were very silly. Particularly so was the raving of one woman. She called us cowards and everything imaginable. She said if she had been there, she would have saved the men. How, she would not tell us. All she would say was that it would have been a simple thing to do. There is one thing that I am sure of, it would be a worse disaster to be tied to a woman like her, than to perish on a burning barge. We learned that there were three men on the barge.

I worked on the tug until spring [1919] and quit, as I wanted to get enough money together to take a trip home. I could not save any money at what I was doing. The trips were too short and there were too many ways to spend money. I left the tug at Galveston.

I joined the *Edgefield*, one of the Shipping Board's ships. It was bound for Antwerp, Belgium. The *Edgefield* was a fine ship, built in Seattle, Washington. It was one of the ninety-day ships. We had a cargo of cotton and grain.

Everything went fine and for the first three or four days out; we were fed the best of food, such as I had not had on any other ship. Chicken, duck, turkey and the choicest of everything that a sailor could desire to eat.

Four days out of Galveston, the freezing plant refused duty. It just would not freeze. All the provisions had to be removed, so the engineer could get at the trouble and fix it. The only place we had to put the provisions was on deck. The weather was very hot, and as it took more than a day to fix the freezing plant, most of the provisions spoiled. Some of the food was put back and refrozen, but when it was cooked and served to us, we could not eat it; therefore, we had no butter or meat for the rest of the trip. As we knew it was not the fault of the captain or the steward, there was not very much complaint.

The Shop Chest aboard the ship had as large a stock of clothing as a small store ashore would carry. The captain and the steward expected to relieve the crew of some of their wages, but they made a mistake in signing on the crew that they did. We were all fitted out in good shape. There also were a number of barrels of bottled near beer that they tried to sell us as real beer. We did not buy any of it as we were bound for a land that had a supply of the real stuff. It was easy to see that the captain was not pleased, for whenever we went to buy tobacco, he would try to sell us other things. When we did not buy, he would say, "You fellows are all alike, you will not buy anything here that would be of some use to you. You all go ashore and throw your money away." I told him one night when he criticized me for not buying, that I worked for my money and would spend it as I saw fit. Whether he liked my answer did not bother me.

We had fine weather all the way across. When we reached the English Channel, we had to take a pilot as there were still some minefields that had not been removed. At Flushing, which is at the mouth of the River Schelde, we dropped the channel pilot and took aboard a Dutch pilot who guided us up the river to Antwerp.

As we steamed up the river, we passed many quaint little villages. The houses, with their thatched roofs just showing above the dike, were indeed a pretty sight. Many of the inhabitants of these villages were standing on the dike watching us go by. The girls with their white caps, white aprons, and wooden shoes looked very pretty, though quaint. Men patrolling the dike, ever on the lookout for a weak spot, made us realize in what a perilous place these people had built their homes.

The farms were laid out as regular as a checkerboard. Old-fashioned windmills were forever pumping to keep the land dry. I could see something strange to me, also very interesting whichever way I looked.

We did not make Antwerp the first day after entering the Schelde River. We spent the night at anchor, as all the traffic on the river is done during the day. Early the following day our ship made fast at the Siberian dock in Antwerp. Antwerp is a very busy port. Its docks are noted as being the finest in the world. Vessels of all descriptions may be seen. Here, I saw my first boat that used a woman for its moving power. The canal boats were drawn by women. They would walk along the edge of the water and tow the boats with a towline. The men would be sitting at the tillers, smoking their long stem pipes. It seemed very funny to me, but I am afraid that the poor women would not see the joke. The canal boats had many children on them. How they could raise the children on the boats and keep them from falling off and drowning was a mystery to me. One day I got a chance to talk to one of the men on a boat that was tied up near our ship. He could speak English. I asked him how they managed to keep the children from falling over board. "Oh!" he replied, "We just spank them." That seemed a simple remedy to me.

I went ashore the first night with a shipmate, Gus Amunsend. We had been shipmates on several ships and we were quite chummy. Gus had been in Antwerp before. He had run away from a Norwegian ship when he was a boy on his first trip away from home, some twenty years earlier. He had made many friends in Antwerp and was anxious to find out if they were still living or if they had been lost in the war.

Some of these friends had run a small café when Gus was there before and sure enough, they were in the same place. They were very glad to see him. It was through them that we saw many interesting places in Antwerp, which in all probability we would not have seen otherwise. They could speak English as well as Gus and me. During the war they had been in England, returning after the Germans had evacuated Antwerp.

These friends took us to see many fine paintings and some of the works of noted sculptures. Our friends were very proud of Van Dyke, Rubens, and other distinguished masters. I must confess that Gus and I did not appreciate the fine works of art as much as we should. We did not understand what it was all about.

We visited the Cathedral of Notre Dame, and it is the most wonderful structure that I have ever seen. Its many aisles and splendid decorations, its large tower, and the many small ones are very beautiful indeed. For a person who is interested and understands art, Antwerp has much to offer them.

Our ship stayed in Antwerp about two weeks. It was two weeks of pleasure for Gus and me. We did not work one full day during that time. We both had money; therefore, the ship was the least of our worry. The rest of our shipmates were not so lucky. They had to stay aboard and work, as they could not draw any money unless they worked.

The captain gave out money very freely at the rate of five francs to the dollar. The exchange was ten francs to the dollar. The captain sure must have been crazy or thought that his crew was. The crew did not say anything about the exchange, but took all the money that they could get. They would wait until we got back to the States and as the captain paid them off, then they would have their say.

Gus and I sure had a wild time. I will never forget one night or should say morning. It was about three o'clock in the morning and daylight when I was sitting on a bench in a small park. I had lost Gus somehow, and I wanted to find him, as we had decided to turn over a new leaf and go aboard the ship to work like good sailors should. Our intentions were good. The park was in a strange part of the city, and the only landmark that I could recognize was the Cathedral spire in the distance.

I went to a place not far from the Cathedral, where I thought I would find Gus. I was disappointed, as the café was closed or I should say it was too early for it to be open. I realized that I was very thirsty. I never wanted a drink so bad in my life. Even water would have been appreciated.

The streets were deserted. I wandered around for probably an hour. I finally saw a man in an American uniform, sitting on a windowsill asleep. As I drew near to him, he heard me and sat up. I went to him and asked if he could tell me where I could get a drink. "I sure can if you have any money. I am broke or I would not be here," he said. I told him that I had money. "Well then," he said, "it looks as if we will get a drink very soon." He went down a passageway and knocked at a door. A man answered and let us in. We followed him up a flight of stairs to a room in which I heard someone talking in English. When we entered the room, whom did I see but Gus. He was talking to another man in uniform like the Good Samaritan I was with.

They had a quart stone jug of gin on the table. "How did you get here?" I asked Gus. "Well," he said, "I was wandering around looking for you when I met my companion, and here I am. How did you get here?" Our two companions were Military Police. They were stationed on that particular street to see that none of the American doughboys entered it. There was too much danger of them breaking the promises that they had made to their wives and sweethearts before leaving home. Uncle Sam wanted his boys to remain true to their loyal ones in the States.

In each house on both sides of the street, for a distance of three or four blocks, there were ten or twelve girls. Those girls were very partial to the American doughboys, if they had money. Uncle Sam took it upon himself to see that those girls did not lead his boys from the straight and narrow way. Sailors, he knew, had a sweetheart in every port and were true to them all, so he did not worry about them.

We soon finished the gin, and I bought a bottle of cognac. By the time it was finished, the cafés were open. We four started out to make a day of it, and it was some day. Everything went along swell until about noon. We four were sitting in a nice little café, listening to a Belgian who was playing on a big accordion, when in walked five Military Police. They ordered our companions to come with them. They were under arrest. Gus and I felt very sorry for them, as we knew it meant the guardhouse.

Gus and I finished the day by taking in all the sailor cafés along Skipper Strasse. About eight o'clock in the evening, we decided to go aboard the ship. The Siberian dock, where our ship lay, was the farthest from the city at that time. It was about four miles, and we were walking. We did not at first find the right road and had that much farther to go. Finally, we found the right road. About a quarter of a mile from the ship, we had to pass an estamente; another name they have for a café. It was the last chance that we had to get a drink before going aboard the ship. We decided to have a nightcap. While sitting at a table having our drink, I said to Gus that I would like to have something to eat. I said eat in Norwegian. It was one of the few words that I knew in the Norse language and it is used a great deal among the sailors.

Two young American soldiers who sat at a table near ours came over to us and started to talk in the Norse language. Gus answered them, but I could not understand much as they jabbered too fast for me. After a few minutes Gus explained to them that I could not understand them, and that all I could say in the Norse, was to ask for something to eat or drink. They talked the rest of the time in English. They were from North Dakota, born of Norwegian parents.

They were stationed nearby to guard a supply depot. They had only been in Antwerp a few days, and that was their first leave; therefore, they were strangers in the city. When Gus and I told them that we were going aboard our ship, they would not hear of it at all. They wanted us to show them around the town. They had plenty of money and were just more than anxious to spend it. I looked on them as two innocent boys abroad, and that it was the duty of Gus and me to see that they did not go too far astray.

Antwerp, I knew, was a dangerous place for two young fellows from North Dakota, that is, if they did not know the ropes. It did not take much persuasion on their part to get Gus and me to retrace our steps into town. We sure did our best to show the boys the sights. I bet they are still talking about that night, if they ever returned to North Dakota. We took in all the places of amusement that we could find, especially dance halls and cafés. We were on the go until daylight. We then chartered a one-horse sea-going cab. It rocked like a ship in a dead swell. We were having a fine time driving from one place to another, stopping quite often for refreshments. Of course the cabby was treated the same as one of us. Everything went fine until afternoon; our cabby became so intoxicated that one of the boys from North Dakota took it upon himself to do the driving. The cabby was in the back seat with us sound asleep. Things went fine for a few blocks until the new driver got it into his head that he could drive better if he rode the horse. He made a big mistake. We had not gone very far, when the Military Police and the Civilian Police marched our two Dakota friends off without any ceremony. The Civilian Police shook the cabby to life and told Gus and me to go, and we lost no time in obeying his orders.

We went to a nearby café to talk the situation over. It did not take us long to decide that the cabby was to blame for it all. Any man that did not have a larger capacity for refreshments than he, had no business to be a cabby. No American cabby would have succumbed so quickly. Gus and I finally decided that we had done enough damage in Antwerp. Two Military Police, two doughboys, and one cabby in the hoosegow were quite enough for us. We went aboard the ship while the going was good. We landed on the ship just before dark, and we were two very tired sailors.

The captain met us as we stepped aboard and what he said would make a book, but I am sure that it would never pass the Board of Censors. As Gus and I were hardened and rather expected it, we were not bothered. We had troubles of a different nature. We were soon in our bunks trying to make up for the sleep that we had lost in the five or six days while we were sightseeing in Antwerp.

When we awakened the next morning, neither of us felt very well and when we sat down to our breakfast and got a whiff of the pork chops that were served us, we felt much worse. Boy, but those pork chops were loud. So loud that they spoiled what desire we did have for food. We decided that if we did not eat that we would not be able to work. I asked one of the sailors, "Do you intend to eat spoiled meat until you get back to the States?" He replied, "I do not want to eat the spoiled meat and while you were ashore, we went to the captain about it. He said that the meat was all right and we could eat it or leave it as we saw fit and that it was all we would get." Gus looked across the table at me and said, "Well, if the old man thinks that we sailors are a lot of hogs, he has another thing coming. What do you say Bill?" "Well," I replied, "if we don't get some fresh meat this ship will sail without me." Gus and four or five more of the sailors agreed with me. Someone suggested that we have a talk with the firemen and see what they thought. They were of the same opinion. Someone got the bright idea and suggested that we go and see the council. I thought that was very good, and if we did not get any results, we at least would get out of another day's work.

I felt very much in need of a drink, so we quickly got into our shore clothes. I took two of the pork chops and wrapped them in a good deal of paper and we started out. The captain met us on deck and wanted to know what we were up to.

When we informed him that we were bound for the council; he said, "If you leave this ship without my permission, I will pay you all off and leave you on the beach here." "Pay off and be damned," we replied. The pay off part did not bother us as one port was the same as another.

It was a long walk to the council, and we made many stops on the way for refreshments. Upon entering the council building, we were informed that the council was busy and would be through in a few minutes.

While we were waiting, my shipmates decided that I had better do the talking. Many of them were not Americans, and some had been going to sea for only a few months. I agreed to do the talking, but if we all landed in the hoosegow, they were not to blame me. We had not waited long when we were told that the council was ready to see us. I had never had any luck with the councils and did not suppose that we would this time. I will say that I had never dealt with a council in person. I had always encountered the vice council or a council agent. But in Antwerp, we saw the council in person.

I explained our grievance to him. We told him how the freezing plant had failed, causing the meat to spoil, and the captain expected us to eat it. Also, that I knew we were entitled to food that was not spoiled. I had hardly finished telling our troubles, when who but the captain came storming in, mad as a March Hare. He never even removed his hat. "Council," he said, "I want to pay them drunken bums off. They are no good, just a lot of lying troublemakers." The council motioned for him to keep still saying, "These men are not drunk and they do not look like bums, nor do I think that they are lying."

Gus looked at the captain and said, "Keep your shirt on and take off your hat." The captain looked as if he was going to have an epileptic fit. He was foaming at the mouth. I knew that the time for me to bring my part of the story to a climax had come. I unwrapped the pork chops and said, "Mr. Council, here is a sample of the meat that we get. It will speak for itself." He took just one whiff, then wrapped it up. He reached for his telephone and called a number. "Is this Surgeon _____? I want you to go aboard the *Edgefield* and inspect the meat." The captain waited for no more. He dashed out the door and was gone.

The council said to us, "Everything will be all right now. I want you to be good boys and go aboard your ship." We thanked him for what he had done and said that we would do as he wished. About two hours after we left the council we returned to the ship. As we came near to the ship, we saw a crowd around the entrance to the freezing room. When we went aboard, we found an army surgeon inspecting the meat. He had a long steel skewer, which he would jab into a piece of meat, pull it out, smell it, and then motion for the steward to dump the meat into the garbage barge that was lying along side. When the surgeon finished, the meat was all dumped. The surgeon went over to the captain and talked to him in a very authoritative manner.

Gus and I had seen and heard enough. We knew that there wasn't any meat aboard and we were hungry, so we went ashore and got something to eat. As that was our last chance to go ashore, because the ship was sailing the next day, we made the best of it. We decided to bid our friends goodbye. We did not return to the ship until the break of day. We had only a few hours to rest before turning to, with a hard day's work ahead of us; getting the ship ready for sea. Well, we got it over somehow. The hatches were all battened down, the deck all cleaned, and we were on our way down the river.

Yes, we got fresh meat, but it was sure tough. Some of the sailors thought it was horsemeat. I don't know, it may have been.

In due time we were steaming through the Channel. We stopped at Portsmouth for oil bunkers, but we were not allowed to go ashore. From the docks where our ship lay, we could see a pub with a big sign, Bass Pale Ale. It was very enticing but there wasn't any chance of our sampling any. Our Antwerp escapade had killed any chance of getting ashore anywhere. In six or eight hours we were on our way, homeward bound, with New Your as our destination.

On the homeward trip, we sailors did not have any trouble. We were all on our best behavior. There was some trouble in the engine room. One of the engineers threw a wrench at one of the oilers and it nearly caused a mutiny. The captain and the chief steward had a row over the Shop Chest. They were mad because the crew would not buy the near beer and shoddy clothing. The captain blamed the steward, and the steward blamed the captain. It ended by the steward being disrated [to reduce or take a rank away]. He had to finish the voyage as a passenger. The ship was sure hoodooed.

I do not like trouble aboard a ship at sea. I was more than glad when we entered the harbor at New York.

Chapter 15
Sailing Ceases

The trouble was not yet over. We, that is the crew, went to the Ferry Building to be paid off. There is where the fun began. We would not accept our pay, as we knew the captain had shortchanged us in Antwerp by giving five francs on the dollar instead of ten the legal exchange.

The commissioner made the captain come through, and it made a difference of over a thousand dollars in the payroll. We got our money all right. I heard afterwards that the captain had to make up the shortage and as he had spent a lot of money on a lady friend while in Antwerp; he was in the hole and the result was that he lost his job.

I was but a few days ashore in New York until I got another ship. I can not recall the name of the ship. It was to go to Buenos Aires with a general cargo. I was to go as quartermaster. It was a very nice ship, good living quarters, and good food. But luck was against me. I was only aboard two days, when a seaman's strike was called. I was very sorry to leave that ship, as I know it would have been a good ship to work on. The officers were all men with plenty of experience, and they had picked up a crew of sailors that would have been good shipmates, but there was nothing else to do but go ashore.

We were nineteen days on the strike, and I enjoyed each and every day of it. There was plenty of excitement. We made a raid on two ships that tried to sail with strikebreakers. They had signed on a crew of West India Negroes. When we finished mauling the Negroes, they had no more desire to go to sea. One day we got a tip that an employment office up on 14th St., a short way west of the Bowery, was getting up a crew for a ship. We marched up there about a thousand strong, raided the office, but the scabs were gone. We took revenge on the office and its fixtures, and ended up by having a game of football down the Bowery with some suitcases that we found in the employment office.

The police of New York sure gave us a good break. They would never show up until we had finished, then they would come and tell us to move on. They would give us either a smile or a wink as they gave the order..

We won the strike. The sailors were to have three watches instead to two. Eight hours instead of twelve on deck. Going to sea with those hours would be more like the life a human being should have. The old watch system did not allow much time for sleep. We also got recognition of our union. Life at sea was much better under the new rules, and I think that a better class of sailors was the result.

They were just starting the bluefishing. As I had always had a desire to make a trip on a fishing boat, and as there was a chance to make some quick money, away I went fishing. Bluefishing is done at night. We fished from dories, two men to a dory. There is lots of excitement to be had at that kind of fishing. Sometimes when the weather was bad, it made me wonder how much a small boat could weather through, but a dory is like a cork.

It was a good thing that I had a good stomach. The bluefish are very game and put up a good fight. But what gives the fishermen a big thrill is when they hook a four or five foot blue shark. We caught several and they are the worst fighters I ever ran across. Many times, especially when the weather was bad, the fishermen cut their line and let the shark go, as the danger of capsizing or swamping the dory was too great. Even when one gets a blue shark into the boat, they thrash around and snap at everything within their reach. I never did like sharks and to be confined with one in a sixteen-foot boat that was jumping around like a cork in a whirlpool gave me the creeps.

I made three trips bluefishing. Each trip took a week to ten days. I made as much money as I would have in two months aboard a ship. The season was drawing to a close, so I quit and joined a ship, called the *Lake Lilicusun* bound for Baltimore to load coal for San Juan, Puerto Rico.

The trip up the Chesapeake was very pleasant. The many towns and villages along its shores were very pretty, but I did not like the Baltimore waterfront. It was so dirty. It did not take us long to load our cargo and we were soon on our way, reaching San Juan early on a very beautiful morning. The island looked like a dream as we steamed into the harbor by the grim Old Spanish Fort. The mountains in the distance, all covered with green vegetation, were indeed beautiful.

The town of San Juan nestling behind the fort, looked very beautiful, and I enjoyed the scene very much. The climate is delightful, hot in the daytime and cool at night. Puerto Rico is directly in the path of the northeast trade winds, so if one can keep out of the sun, it is very pleasant.

The natives are a much better class than those I saw in Cuba. I don't think there is as much mixed bloods in Puerto Rico. The natives seem to be more of a pure Spanish.

There were signs of poverty everywhere. Many of the children looked half starved, and they were all the time begging food or money from the ships. They were like fish in the water. We would throw pennies in the water and they would dive for them, never missing a penny. It was very amusing to watch them. Our ship was surrounded with these young divers. When we left, there wasn't any small change left on board our ship. I suppose they are still watching for another ship with more "loco Americanos" on board. If not those same divers, you will find others of a younger generation.

We discharged our cargo of coal and went right to Jucaro, Cuba to load sugar. Jucaro is situated on the southeast coast of Cuba, on the bay of Bueno Esperanza.

Our ship was anchored a mile out from shore. The cargo was brought out to the ship in lighters. The stevedores were mostly from Haiti. A more mongrel looking lot of humans, I have never seen. They were of all shades, from yellow to jet black. A worse lot of thieves I don't believe ever lived. They would have stolen the ship, if we had not had the anchor out. It took about a week to get our load and from captain down to mess boy, we were glad when we sailed away.

We had fine weather until we got north of the Bahama Islands. From there north we hit bad weather. Strong northerly winds delayed us so much that we had to go into Norfolk, Virginia for coal. We arrived at Norfolk with but coal enough for four or five hours' steam. We soon had the needed coal loaded and were on our way bound for Boston. We encountered bad weather from the start, and the farther north we got it grew worse. When we were off the Massachusetts coast, the weather was so bad that we had to heave to for twenty-four hours. The sea was running mountain high. That our little ship ever rode through it was a miracle. At times, it looked as if we would surely be swamped. A big sea would lift us high up in the air like a cork, then the bottom would drop out of everything. Down, down we would go into the trough of the sea. It seemed like going down into a big valley. Then a big wall of water would suddenly loom up before us. It looked as if it was going to engulf us, but our good little ship would raise her bow, and the monstrous wall of water would slide under us. Many times, we were not so fortunate. We would rise with the wave all right, but if it had a white cap, the comber would break over our ship's bow and bury the ship to midship. Then, like a water spaniel she would raise and shake off the surplus water, much to the relief of everyone on board. We were very heavily loaded and extremely lucky to have weathered through, as there were several ships lost in that storm, and many ships were severely damaged. Beyond delaying us, we suffered no damage. We reached Boston finally and were paid off. I then started on one of the most exciting journeys of my life: I was going home.

You may think that there isn't anything exciting about going home, but put yourself in my place. It had been nearly twenty years since I had left home, just a rosy faced boy, and I was returning a very much weather-worn man. I wondered if everything at home had changed as much as I had. I also wondered how I would find those I had left behind.

My first jump was to New York. I had left some money in a bank in New York, and I also expected some mail. A few hours after my arrival in New York, I was ready to make my final dash. When I bought my ticket at Grand Central Station through to Chicago, I was more excited than when I signed on the *Endurance* for the voyage to the Antarctic.

When once aboard the train, steaming up the Hudson with New York City dropping out of sight, I had a feeling that I was not only leaving New York behind but also my happy-go-lucky, carefree and easy life. Something seemed to tell me that I was about to start out on a new and strange life. The trip to Chicago was soon over. It was not the Chicago I knew as a boy. The noisy old cable cars had disappeared. The streets were all strange to me and as there were so many skyscrapers, I recognized only a few places. The last forty miles of my journey to the town of Joliet, from which I had started out in quest of my fortune (that I never made), was made in the dark. I was not able to see what changes had been made during my absence. It was when I stepped off the train that I realized one big change had been made.

Instead of the little old red station with its two waiting rooms, one for women and one for men with the ticket office in between, there was a fine Union Station, built to accommodate the several railroads that run through the town. When I walked out on to the street, for once in my life I will have to admit that I was lost. I did not know which way to turn. I was as much at sea as Columbus was when he was forty days out from Spain. I could not recognize a thing. Modern buildings replaced the old landmarks. I can sympathize with Rip Van Winkle. I know just how he must have felt after his twenty-year snooze.

I hailed a cab. The man who runs the taxi cabs now is the son of the man who owned the old horse cabs. Before I had time to get over the first surprise, I was giving my parents the biggest surprise of their lives. They were not expecting me for a few months. I received a very cordial welcome, as a prodigal son generally does.

The comforts of a home that I had not known for many years seemed very strange to me at first, but I soon became accustomed to them. As my parents did not want me to go away again, I settled down to the work-a-day life.

Of course, in due time the right girl came along and then said yes to the questions asked by the Sky Pilot and signed on the Ship called *Matrimony* for a life-long cruise. After awhile, one more joined the crew, a little brown-eyed baby girl.

My ramblings are done now in the way of dreams during the evenings, in the good ship *Easy Chair.*

Well, that bus is stopping. Here is where I get off. So long. [57]

---

[57] See Preface.

Epilogue
"A Bird's-Eye View of Dad's Life"

by Elizabeth Anna Balewell Rajala

My father, William Lincoln Bakewell, began his adventurous life soon after he learned to walk. I remember my grandmother telling me that when her two sons went out to play, my father was soon gone, heading down the streets of Joliet, Illinois to see what was new and interesting.

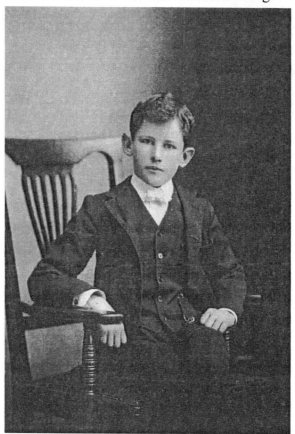

William Lincoln Bakewell

Taken before he turned 11 and before he left home.
It was the last picture taken as a child.

When he was 7, he had ridden the rails for 100 miles before he was caught and returned home to Joliet, Illinois. By the advanced age of 11, this independent kid had traveled by boxcar to southeast Missouri and eastern Kansas—where he worked on farms. Most of the time spent in Missouri was in the area that the town of Sikeston is today. Dad spoke of alligators living in the swampy areas. Of course, they are long gone today. This trip took about two years. My dad returned home with a fever, believing he might have malaria.

My father mentioned little about his life as a boy. His father worked in the steel mills located there in Joliet. Dad spoke fondly of his grandparents, especially about the day he brought a newspaper home relating the death of Queen Victoria of England. His mother and grandmother ran to the bedroom and carried on for hours. No one would tell my dad why the household was so extremely upset. Rumor was that the grandmother was connected to the royalty—of course, never proven to this day.

School was not a favorite place for my dad. In those days, white ruffled shirts were worn. He wanted the blue chambray shirts that the "blue collar" workers wore. Dad did mention the Ridgewood School. He always wanted to leave and explore the geographical areas mentioned. The only teacher, he spoke of with some fondness was a very petite feisty woman that ruled with an "iron hand." Even the parents did not cross this "bantam rooster."

As a lad, Dad had a favorite uncle, William Edward Lincoln. This William was my dad's mother's youngest brother. Uncle Bill was about 10 years older than my father. From this partnership and at a very young age my father obtained many teenage "facts." The one that lasted a lifetime was smoking.

My father did mention that as a lad living in Joliet, there was much separation of nationalities. Language and religion were often the barriers.

At the tender age of 15 he started his 20 years of continuous adventures. He rode the rails north for several days. A cold February day of 1904 found him suffering from cold and hunger. Also found by the brakeman who sent him flying off the train in Seney, a small town in the Upper Peninsula of Michigan.

After a man befriended him with food, Dad started working his way north from one lumber camp to another. These experiences began his education in cooperation and survival. Finally he was in the area of Spragge, Ontario, Canada. After this lumber camp he trekked north through the Canadian wilderness looking for the Canadian Pacific Railroad. He intermittently rode the rails and worked his way west.

He dropped down into Montana and worked on Milroy's ranch and trapped for several years. He kept going west until land ran out. He was in San Francisco, California when his sailing days began. Never having sailed, he signed on the *Philadelphia* in January 1914 as an able seaman. This voyage took him around Cape Horn and up the east coast of South America and across the Atlantic to the British Isles. Several ships later found him on the *Golden Gate* leaving Newport, Wales for Montevideo, Uruguay. The *Golden Gate* was the flag ship through the new locks at Newport, Wales. Fortunately or unfortunately, the *Golden Gate* hit the breakwater at Montevideo. This put the sailors out of work. My dad and two other sailors crossed the River Plata into Buenos Aires, Argentina. There in the harbor was the *Endurance*. My dad saw the ship and fell in love with it, not knowing where this ship was going. He inquired about a job, saying he was an able seaman. Now he knew it was the ship for Sir Ernest Shackleton's Imperial Trans-Antarctic Expedition. He was one of 5000 applicants (most of these were interviewed in England) and only 25 were chosen. The plan was to dogsled across Antarctica. Needless to say, he had no idea about the forthcoming adventure. So began the epic adventure of surviving two years on the ice with the

Shackleton Expedition in the Weddell Sea off the coast of Antarctica. One might say the adventure of a lifetime and a miracle that all 28 men returned alive.

Like most of the crew aboard Shackleton's 1914-1916 expedition to cross Antarctica, which failed due to ice crushing the ship, my father spoke little of the ordeal, but the story is slowly becoming one of the world's most inspiring sagas of endurance, courage, and leadership. My father with the help of Walter How stowed Perce Blackborow aboard, saving his life more than once, and began a lifelong friendship with the family.

The *Endurance* sailed into the Weddell Sea and became beset in the ice. The crew spent the winter somewhat comfortably in the ship. Spring came with increased movement of the seas. This caused presure ice (house-size) to batter the ship. Soon the ship could not withstand the pressure and Shackleton gave the order to abandon ship. Now life and survival began on the ice. Over five months was spent on ice floes. The 28 men were crowded into five small tents with limited amounts of food. How and Dad waded through the icy waters, filling the crushed *Endurance,* trying to retrieve items and came upon the room that had some of Hurley's invaluable photographs and brought them out.

The *Weddell Sea* is somewhat horseshoe shaped and this causes the currents to circle north, carrying ice and men northward to warmer waters. Now the 28 men had to take to the three small lifeboats. Five or six days later, they saw their last survival hope—Elephant Island. This inhospitable island had very few safe landing places. Finally, they found one. This island is a penguin rookery and even the penguins do not stay all year. The significance of penguins leaving meant the continuous source of food was gone.

The only source of rescue was to sail the *22-foot James Caird* over 800 miles to South Georgia. McNish, How and my father and those able to help, sewed the canvas bags for ballast and the canvas decking that would withstand the pounding waters when at sea. Shackleton and five others sailed the *James Caird* on this two-week trip to South Georgia (a small island with several whaling sations). This trip would cross the most dangerous ocean waters in the world.

My dad and 21 others spent 4 ^{1}/2 months on Elephant Island awaiting rescue.

One would think that this was enough adventure, but NO. My dad ranched in Argentina and then went back to sea during WWI. He sailed on the Merchant Marine ships that hauled cargo to England, France, and Belgium for the soldiers. Two of the ships were torpedoed but the crews were rescued.

Finally, after more adventures, he returned to Joliet, Illinois and took up railroading.

My father married Elma Merle Potter in 1925. An only child, I, Elizabeth Anna, was born in 1927. Around this time he had a boat, the *Shamrock,* on the Des Plaines River and the Illinois Canal, in which he transported people and cargo for various businesses. Later, he worked full-time on the Rock Island Railroad in Joliet and the Diesel Electric Plant in LaGrange, Illinois.

E. Merle PotterBakewell and
William Bakewell — 1925

There in Illinois we lived on a three acre farm, raising chickens, milk goats, pigs, and garden vegetables, Also, we had cherry trees. On rented land, corn, oats, and asparagus were grown. This farm was on US 30 highway (also known as Lincoln Highway) between Joliet and Plainfield, Illinois.

The Shamrock—Bakewell's boat on the Desplaines River and the Illinois Canal. Boat is docked at Joliet, Illinois.
Time—circa 1925

Due to the depression, dad's parents moved in with us. Times were hard and families had to do a lot of sharing and became very thrifty. Many people were put out of work and paychecks were cut in half for those that did work. The depression ended but WWII started. Rationing cards became the new way of life causing gas, food, and clothing limitations. The war ending led to my dad's next adventure.

Michigan Central Tower, Rock Island Railroad,
Joliet, Illinois
William L. Bakewell—Towerman

My dad's last great adventure was relocating the family to Dukes, Michigan in August of 1945. All the household and farm possessions were loaded into a boxcar, my father as well, for the long trip north. (He had wanted to move to Alaska, but my mother had drawn the line, "NO.") My mother and I and a young friend, Don Woske drove the Dodge pick-up towing a Model A. Ford (all loaded to the hilt) to Michigan. As I was the only licensed driver, most of the 16 hours of driving was done by me. We experienced

William L. Bakewell playing with "Billy," the billy goat. This three acre farm was 5 miles West of Joliet on US 30.

one flat tire in Menominee, Michigan. Having no spare (World War II was just over and no tires available) the garage attendant fixed the inner tube and put a boot in the tire. By the way, it took the boxcar three days to find its way to Dukes.

In Dukes, my parents had a dairy farm until the 1953 tornado took the top part of the barn. Then they switched to sheep.

They continued farming until my father was in his late 70s. Both parents were active in Farm Bureau. My dad proudly remained a Masonic Lodge member for life. In younger days, my mother belonged to the Eastern Star.

Evenings were mostly spent at home with their favorite pastime of reading. My dad did have another hobby in his old age. He had a small sawmill and ran it with his friend, Sam Winters.

My dad was active until his death in May of 1969. My mother pasted away in June of 1974.

Dukes, Michigan—The Dairy Farm that Bakewells moved to in 1945. The top of the barn was taken away by a tornado in June of 1953. Cows were then sold.

Needless to say, I grew up with a great knowledge of geography and a yen to travel. Much of the traveling had to wait until after my marriage to Waino Rajala. After we were married we spent the first 3 ^{1}/2 months traveling through many of the western states. Over the years we reached all 50 states. Even as we worked (farming, teaching, and railroading) and raised three daughters, we found time to travel in the states and Canada.

William L. Bakewell and his sheep farming after the tornado. Bottom part of the barn was still usable. Raised sheep for 10 years.

Waino's parents were born in Finland, so in 1970 we made our first of several trips to Finland to visit the relatives. Also, we included the British Isles as several of the families of the *Endurance* crew lived there.

In 1964, my dad and I had attended the 50th year celebration of the sailing of the *Endurance*. Six of the *Endurance* crew were in attendance. Lord Edward Shackleton (second son of Sir Ernest Shackleton) hosted the event.

Sadly to say, Waino died in 1987. Thus it was 1999 before my daughters, Sarah and Nina, and I had the opportunity to sail to the Antarctic. Luckily we did not get beset in the ice but did experience a force 12 hurricane.

The ice formations are beautiful and like snowflakes with no two alike. One 200 foot tall iceberg was 32 miles long

(B10A) and we paralleled it for many hours. When the sun hits the icebergs, it is a spectacular site. The colors, shapes and the designs that the water makes by washing away the soft ice creates an artist's dream.

E. Merle & William L. Bakewell with Shep—1953.
They were Dairy Farmers until the tornado.

The sea life consists of elephant seals, fur seals, Weddell seals, leopard seals and sometimes whales.

"A Bird's-Eye View of Dad's Life"

Many birds live in the Antarctic area, namely: terns, skuas, albatross, and several kinds of penguins. Penguins are quite curious and will come up to you if you stand still.

When tourists travel to the Antarctic, they are encouraged to leave nothing but footprints and are not to take anything. Even the many scientific stations are extremely careful not to pollute or damage the fragility of the continent.

We spent about 45 minutes on Elephant Island and it hasn't changed one bit since 1916.

One thing to remember is that the ice at the Arctic and Antarctic plays an important role in keeping much of the hot areas of the globe livable.

Grandpa Bakewell's genes have also been passed to Sarah, Mary and Nina. All of the granddaughters have done various amounts of traveling and continue to do so.

Traveling (next to reading) is the greatest way to get a first hand education.

With the help of many, I have tried to put my dad's memoirs in a publishable form. I have footnoted the memoirs in many places. In no way during the editing have my daughters or I changed my dad's story or his way of expressing and relating his adventures. The footnoting was done to enhance and explain situations that readers may not be familiar with at this time.

My Hero, Will

by Matthew W. Roop

My name is Matthew Roop. I had the great fortune of sharing a portion of my life with William Bakewell and his wife Merle on their farm in the Upper Peninsula of Michigan. The influence of this man in my life remains to this day.

The Bakewell's befriended my family shortly after we moved to Dukes, which was little more than a crossroads with a combination post office/gas station. We enjoyed fresh brown eggs, garden vegetables and most of all friendly conversation in their warm farmhouse kitchen. By way of this friendship, I was allowed the privilege of helping with farm chores after school and on weekends.

Will, as he was known by his friends, was incredibly vital for a man in his seventies and I, a large strapping lad of 13 years, performed just a small fraction of the work he was able to accomplish. Will was a man who lived in the here and now and stories of his travels and adventures would only occasionally come up in conversation. When he chose to recount an event of his past, I hung on every word. The adventures and travels of an able seaman on tall sailing ships to the ends of the earth were beyond my comprehension but mesmerizing and fascinating. My nagging for more led to Will allowing me to read his manuscript of the voyage and subsequent ordeal of being ship wrecked in the Antarctic for 14 months.

The book you are now reading is a factual account of Will's experiences of this exploration. Above all, William Bakewell, in my personal experience was an honest and virtuous man. He was not superfluous or prone to exaggeration and none is contained herein.

I had many fond memories of Will and Merle. The first "short" cup of coffee, my first car, a 1955 Chevy which Will took me for a ride in at 90 miles per hour to show me "the old girl still had some get up and go left in her." The perturbed but loving look I would get from Merle when she would insistently try to pay me for chores (I would hide the money under the sugar bowl for her to find the next morning). One Saturday, Will told me to "play hooky" from chores and go fishing. I returned muddy, bloody, and proud as a peacock with a few small brook trout, which Merle applauded, prepared and served, even though she had already made a big pot of stew. Sitting in the kitchen near the coal fired stove while Will hand rolled a cigarette, of which I never saw him smoke more than a couple in the course of a day, and explaining the excessive use of tobacco and alcohol was the road to ruin. Also, watching him without complaint, put on his rain gear, and go out into a torrential rainstorm, to get the sheep in the barn, while he said "Sheep aren't too smart but most have enough sense to come in out of the rain. If it's a sudden downpour like this, a couple might be laying down and get waterlogged and too heavy to stand up by themselves. Once I haul them to their feet, they head for the barn. Better for me to get wet than give the coyotes a free meal."

There is no doubt in my mind that many men, also owe their very lives to William Bakewell. His rifle which was vital in procuring game, skills as a seaman, selfless compassion and indefatigable spirit, made him as valuable to his shipmates as he was to me personally.

The feat that this man was the only American participant of a "British" exploration and quickly earned the respect and admiration of his comrades, speaks volumes to what an exceptional individual that he was.

I wish to thank Elizabeth Rajala, daughter of Will and Merle Bakewell, for allowing me to give you a glimpse of her father's life, as seen through the eyes of a 13-year-old boy. I owe a large part of my love of reading, history, nature, and adventure to William Bakewell. To this great explorer, adventurer, and human being, I am eternally grateful.

Matthew W. Seiy

Acknowledgements

My family has given tremendous support and encouragement to me. Without said support, this manuscript may never have come to fruition. I especially want to thank Sarah and Nina for all their computer expertise and chapter title assistance. My appreciation goes to Sarah's husband, James, daughters, Kristen and Stephanie who gave invaluable help. Nina's husband, John, has been behind the scenes with pertinent information. I deeply appreciate Mary's artistic ability and thank her for the outline maps and especially the train sketch. Also, thanks to Mary's husband, John, and sons, Zackery and Lance for their personal support.

All beginnings have to have endings if completed. This exclusive thanks goes to Violet and Robert Hall (cousins) for helping me complete the project. Without the Hall's, I am sure the end never would have been attained.

Many other friends and acquaintances have assisted in numerous ways. Those I want to most of all thank are: Rand Shackleton, Laura M. Chaney, James Carter, Allen Acker, Caryl Dawson, Ben Garrett, David Huisman, Matthew Roop, Margaret Hudacko, Mary Jayne Hallifax, The Public /School Librarians, Lynne Hadley, Jack McRae, Scott Polar Research Institute (especially Lucy Martin), Grand Marais Historical Society (Michigan), Steve Robinson of *Sea Breezes'* magazine (Isle of Man), and Wells Chapin of Avery Color Studios for all his advice.

For anyone that I have neglected to mention, I truly thank you from the bottom of my heart.

Also, thanks to the many books and people that I have read or had discussions with, as I know this has expanded my knowledge and enhanced my wisdom.

Elizabeth Anna Bakewell Rajala

William Bakewell's Chronological Dates

1888, Nov. 26	Birth of William Lincoln Bakewell
1904, Feb	Bakewell rode boxcars from Joliet, Illinois to Seney, Michigan
1905 – 1908	North to the Canadian Pacific Railroad and west
1908 – 1912	Montana area and ranching
1912 – 1913	West again—San Francisco
1914, Jan.	Able Seaman aboard the *Philadelphia*
1914, Oct.	*Golden Gate* hit breakwater at Montevideo, Uruguay, South America
1914 – Oct. 26	Joined the *Endurance* at Buenos Aires, Argentina
1914, Oct to 1916, Aug.	Antarctic trip with Sir Ernest Shackleton on *Endurance*
1915 – Oct. 27	Left beset *Endurance*. Life on ice began
1915, Nov. 21	Crushed ship sank.
1916, Apr. 19	Took to lifeboats for five days to Elephant Island
1916, Apr. 28	*James Caird* sailed with six men to South Georgia.
1916, Aug. 30	*Yelcho* rescued the 22 men on Elephant Island.
1916, Oct.	Ranching life in Patagonia, Argentina
1917, Late	Back to sea for WWI.
1923, Late	Returned to Joliet, Illinois. He returned to sea for a short time.
1923 – to about 1930	Purchased and sailed *Shamrock* on Illinois Canal and Desplaines River.
1925, Feb. 19	Married Elma Merle Potter
1925 – 1945	Worked on Rock Island Railroad and Diesel Motor Plant
1927, Oct.	Daughter, Elizabeth Anna was born.
1945, Aug	Used boxcar to move to Dukes, Michigan
1945 – 1969	Farmed, dairy and sheep
1969, May	Deceased
1999, Nov. 26	Elizabeth (daughter) and Sarah and Nina (granddaughters) traveled to Antarctica, Elephant Island, and South Georgia to retrace part of William Bakewell's journey.

The Bakewell Team

This team made this book possible.

Sarah Rajala, Mary Severson, and Nina Rajala

Elizabeth Rajala and Violet Hall